STEP ON THE CRACKS

STEP ON THE CRACKS

REINVENTING HAPPINESS,
POSITIVITY, AND OPTIMISM

BRANDON POSIVAK

NEW DEGREE PRESS

COPYRIGHT © 2020 BRANDON POSIVAK

STEP ON THE CRACKS

Reinventing Happiness, Positivity, and Optimism

ISBN   978-1-63676-407-8

CONTENTS

———

For my grandfather, you showed me the true power of extending happiness and positivity to those around me. For my Uncle Michael, you showed me less really is more, and sometimes the simplest answer is the right one. For Mark Hoffman, you taught me how to be accountable and to visualize and pursue my goals. Your legacy will live on, and your message will forever be immortalized in the words on these pages. For my family and friends, each of you positively impacted me, and this book was possible because you helped me believe in myself and find my voice. With this book and during every day of my life, I thank you.

NOTE FROM THE
AUTHOR

—

Dear Cherished Reader,

Playing tag under the streetlights with friends, sharing chili cheese fries at Islands Restaurant with my dad, and playing Deal or No Deal at a Dave N' Busters arcade—these moments defined my childhood happiness. As I got older, moments which made me happy changed to going to the beach, going fishing with friends, and spending time with my family. I found accomplishing my goals made me happy. My ambition grew as I worked toward attaining my personal, academic, and athletic goals.

In those moments, I felt free. My worries no longer existed, and I could just exhale. I wanted the feeling that came with achieving my goals and spending time with family and friends to be a part of my everyday life, or at least more frequently than moments of isolated memory.

In the years since my childhood, I have learned each person has their own unique concept of happiness—their unique "happiness fingerprint." I also learned not all happiness is considered equal. In his best-selling book *Stumbling on Happiness*, Harvard Psychology Professor Daniel Gilbert explains human beings are the only beings on the planet who can actually create happiness for ourselves. Through our frontal lobe, we have the ability to create synthetic happiness to make us happy during a difficult time.[1]

The happiness I felt as a child from participating in certain events seemed easy and effortless, but it was both finite and temporary. Those moments were not enough to fuel a happy life. So I decided to search for a more authentic, purer version of happiness. That's when things got complicated. During my senior year of college, I gave up playing Division I college baseball to come home and help multiple family members with their illnesses. I began working full-time along with taking a full course load. It was difficult to see my friends enjoying their senior year at school and making the most of their final year of collegiate athletics.

I was at home helping my family in any way I could to catalog as many mental images as possible of my grandfather and uncle before they passed. Happiness was at a premium.

After extensive research on happiness, positivity, and optimism, I could look back on my experiences through a new lens. I had a new language to identify the feelings I struggled

---

1   Daniel Gilbert, *Stumbling on Happiness* (New York: Random House, 2007).

to verbally express. While this research was interesting and began turning the wheels in my mind about the different levels of happiness, there was still a missing piece: how to apply this to my personal life. The motivational speakers and psychological experiments I studied focused on the lives of adults and how they make their lives more fulfilling. I found very little information on my generation, Generation Z, or those born between 1996 and 2009 according to *Pew Research.*[2]

Generation Z is also known as "post-Millennials" and the "iGeneration." As I sifted through information on how to be happy, I realized the majority of information I came across on Google regarding Gen Z was geared toward "employers hiring Gen Z candidates" or "marketers branding toward Gen Z consumers."

I struggled to relate to the psychologists and authors from other generations discussing Gen Z psychology and emotional fortitude because no matter how well intentioned and influential their work is, they are not in our shoes. At a crucial time in our lives, while we are becoming the newest young members of the working world and making the transition into adulthood, happiness is getting lost among conversations about careers, responsibilities, and future success. We are the new members of the job market, and we are taking on new responsibilities and creating new expectations. In all this, we still want to find happiness.

---

2   Michael Dimock, "Defining Generations: Where Millennials End and Generation Z Begins," *Pew Research Center,* January 17, 2019.

Each generation before us has experienced a similar transition when entering the real world, but there are ways in which our generation differs from earlier ones. Our childhoods were immersed in technology and social media, and we are entering a job market dramatically different from even a generation ago.

Because of technology and social media, Gen Z now has opportunities different from our grandparents, parents, and even older siblings. As a member of Generation Z, I was eight years old when Apple released the first MacBook and nine years old when they released the first iPhone. I grew up with commercials for the iPod Nano and iPod Shuffle, which allowed users to put all their favorite music onto one device. I'm a member of the generation who had DVD players set into the backs of seats in SUVs and Bluetooth built into the dashboard of cars.

I got my first cell phone at age eleven, my first Facebook account at age thirteen, and my first Instagram and Snapchat accounts at age fourteen. I grew up socializing with my friends after school through Club Penguin, Farmville, Minecraft, and Call of Duty. We could text each other to set up our own play dates, and we could Facetime each other if we wanted a face-to-face conversation.

Through my Facebook account, I could share funny videos and play games with my friends. I could post pictures to share memories with everyone in my network on Instagram. Through social media, I could stay updated on events from around the world and share my thoughts and memories with my friends. Friends and family were a click away, which has an impact on our happiness as a generation.

Millennials grew up seeing Tom from MySpace when they set up an account, the Game Boy was the premiere hand-held gaming system, and Beanie Babies slowly became an international collector's item. Gen X saw VHS videos, made mixtapes of songs to listen to on repeat, and *Charles in Charge* lunchboxes scattered the playground. Baby Boomers saw Rock Hudson and Dorris Day as Hollywood's great acting duo, *Turner Classic Movies* had not become classics yet, and Walter Cronkite was the news. The Silent Generation saw television go from black and white to color, jukeboxes become a staple in every diner, and the first synthetic rubber tires made for cars.

Each generation is unique in their own right with certain "calling cards" to relate to. Generation Z is no different.

I learned standing out in a unique way was important. My parents, teachers, and coaches always said I had to work hard to differentiate myself from the pack. I heard about kids with a 4.0 GPA and an impressive résumé failing to get into premier colleges. I heard about teenagers who were starting their own hedge funds, building villages for impoverished families in Africa, and starting successful businesses. I constantly felt the pressure to achieve and stand out.

But through it all, happiness still became more elusive as I got older. Social cliques formed online and I thought more about how many likes I got than why I was posting in the first place. My online reputation and persona seemed like the ultimate factor in the way someone my age viewed me, and a good reputation and social media following was a sign of success.

So I tried to find myself and my identity. In doing so, my views on technology, social media, and my own expectations shifted. Happiness got lost in the mix of my desire to accomplish and to check all the boxes, and the feeling of eating chili cheese fries with my dad at Islands Restaurant became a distant memory.

Whether I liked it or not, I was growing up, and I wanted to find a way to combine happiness with my academic, athletic, and professional goals.

As I began to research more about the foundations of happiness, I came across a quote by Denis Waitley, the author of *Seeds of Greatness,* who describes it perfectly. He says, "Happiness cannot be traveled to, owned, earned, or worn. It is the spiritual experience of living every minute with love, grace and gratitude."[3]

My paternal grandfather, Pop-Pop, taught me what it meant to have a positive and optimistic outlook each day. His wife, my grandmother, died when I was four, and he has lived by himself in the house my dad grew up in for the past seventeen years.

I thought of him when I wanted to learn more about happiness because of his unrelenting persistence and control over

---

3   Denis Waitley, *Seeds of Greatness: Ten Best-kept Secrets of Total Success,* (Ringwood, Victoria: Brolga Publications, 1994).

his life. He is in his mid-eighties, and even after multiple surgeries, he still lifts weights and goes swimming every day. He volunteers every week as an usher at his church and drives patients at the local hospital to their doctor's appointments if they can no longer drive.

To this day, he makes me laugh when he mixes Hungarian with English and uses words—his "Pop-Popisms"—not quite found in Webster's dictionary. He always makes me smile when he yells at the TV during a sports game and says the coach is a bum. Despite the hardships he's endured—fighting in the Vietnam War and losing his wife at a young age—Pop-Pop hangs on to a positive, optimistic attitude.

Pop-Pop always reminds me of a quote by Winston Churchill: "The positive thinker sees the invisible, feels the intangible, and achieves the impossible." To me, having a positive attitude is like possessing a superpower, and Churchill's quote sums up the power of positivity and optimism.

Pop-Pop puts the happiness of others before his own, and he is a big reason why I strive to be a positive person each and every day.

He and my dad would always talk about serendipity. They said, "sometimes the best things happen when you don't expect them to and when you stop trying so hard to make them happen." This was followed by a mantra he taught to my dad, who passed it on to me: "Keep your head where your feet are."

Pop-Pop showed me as tempting as it is to think about the future, staying in the present and finding a way to create good in the world will keep you grounded in reality. He also showed me though it is easy to point out what went wrong and what could be better, and even though it's hard to find the positives in each situation, we should always strive to see them.

This idea of perspective is elaborated upon by Harvey Mackay, the author of *Swim with the Sharks Without Being Eaten*. He says, "When you wake up every day, you have two choices. You can either be positive or negative; an optimist or a pessimist. I choose to be an optimist. It's all a matter of perspective."[4]

A positive outlook for me is *stepping on the cracks*. The idea of *step on the cracks* began when I was young. I always loved to play games (and still do), but there was one game in particular I played almost every day. I was the only player in the game, I could play virtually anywhere, and no one around knew I was playing. Perhaps the best part was there was no set up or clean up, and I could play as many times as I wanted to.

This game had just one simple rule: don't step on any cracks in the sidewalk or lines in the cross walk. I told myself they were lava, and if I touched them I would get burned and lose the game. If I stepped on a crack with one foot, that foot was now burned, and I would only use my other foot to hop across the crosswalk and complete the game. So I had to avoid the cracks at all costs to win the game.

---

4   Harvey Mackey and Kenneth H. Blanchard, *Swim with the Sharks: Without Being Eaten Alive* (London: Sphere, 2013).

Innocent enough, right? Well, the game became more prevalent and evolved as I got older. I found myself expanding the game inside my house and school, and any building I walked into was now a playground. I avoided stepping on the cracks in the wooden floor panels in my house and the colored hallway tiles of my school. However, what had started as a game slowly became somewhat of a compulsion.

It got to the point where I would be walking and while I was mid-conversation with a friend, I would awkwardly step short or elongate my stride suddenly to miss a crack on the sidewalk. It was so engrained into my brain it didn't even seem like a conscious choice anymore.

It was a steadfast rule, and there were no exceptions. I took it so seriously that anywhere I walked, no matter how preoccupied I was, I found myself always remaining conscious of the cracks on the ground.

While in college, I slowly began to recognize I was setting up impossible expectations for myself which were completely unnecessary. No one was forcing me to have this rule of never stepping on the cracks. It was my sole creation. It used to be a fun childhood game, but now it felt like a job.

During my junior year of college, I was walking and avoiding the cracks on the sidewalk per usual, but I stepped too far forward and hit a patch of black ice. I immediately lost my balance and fell forward onto the icy concrete. Luckily, I wasn't hurt. However, this was a wakeup call. I wanted to finally end the game for good. This rule I had in my head since I was a kid no longer served its purpose, and it had become a detriment to my happiness.

So that night I wanted to make the change. I was alone on the sidewalk, staring at the cracks glistening with the salt crystals on the walkways, and I lifted my foot and stepped down onto the first crack despite a voice in my head screaming not to. I walked down the entire sidewalk not looking down or worrying about where my shoes hit.

I continued this until it became a habit and my mind was free. I had stepped out of the mental prison cell I had created.

Now whenever I feel mentally locked up or frustrated, I remind myself to *step on the cracks*. I felt like I had finally broken through that mental barrier. In writing this book, I wanted to emphasize the importance of mental equanimity as we go through life.

Telling myself to *step on the cracks* is a constant reminder to keep my mind free and clear. We all have a phrase, a quote, or even a single word which speaks to us and keeps us grounded in the moment, and we can use this to spur our action.

Positivity is an active choice we make through our perspective. A positive outlook does not directly translate to personal happiness, but it is a step in affecting those around you in a positive way.

I took this idea with me as I immersed myself in my psychological research on what makes human beings happy and why. In every single thing I've ever done, I always wanted to be the best.

"Do today what others won't, so tomorrow you can do what others can't."—Jerry Rice

I was ready to run through brick walls and scale mountains to earn the success and recognition I desired. I wanted to separate myself from the pack, to be a household name, and feel as though I achieved my full potential. As I got older that desire grew, and I knew I needed to find a direction for my unrelenting ambition.

When my mom was struggling with her parents' illnesses, her friends said, "you deserve to be happy." Similarly, when I left school to come home and help my family, some of my friends expressed similar thoughts. In both cases, my mom's friends and my friends were trying to help us through a difficult time in our lives by reminding us happiness was still possible.

However, I thought about that phrase as I continued in my research on happiness, positivity, and optimism, and it seemed more like a gift someone would give me than something I would achieve on my own. My family, my friends, and my hobbies were all external sources, and they gave me the gift of happiness. I knew the phrase was meant to conjure hope for the future, but I wanted to do my part in willing that happiness to occur in the present as well.

The phrase implies if I am perceived by others as a good person, if I help people, and if I put the thoughts of others before my own, then I deserve to be happy. With this "if then" phrase, happiness becomes a reward for your actions if you check all the boxes. But instead of believing I *deserve* to be happy, I resolved to be proactive in how I could attain the happiness I desire.

After making the conscious decision to be happy, I changed my perspective and recognized happiness isn't something I pursue. I no longer felt a need to avoid stepping on the cracks in life. I was no longer in a mental prison.

We control our minds, and we control how we affect others with our actions. As human beings we are self-aware, and we can, in turn, make the conscious choice to affect others in a positive way. That is a powerful gift each of us can give. When social media, technological advances, and the pressures of the professional world are overwhelming, remember this unique power we possess.

As author of *The Light in the Heart: Inspirational Thoughts for Living Your Best Life* Roy T. Bennett says, "Be the reason someone smiles. Be the reason someone feels loved and believes in the goodness in people."[5] To my fellow members of Gen Z, let's choose to make a positive change in our world, and with our unique abilities, step on the cracks.

Sincerely Yours,
Brandon Posivak

---

5   Roy T. Bennett, *The Light in the Heart: Inspirational Thoughts for Living Your Best Life* (Roy T. Bennett, 2016).

CHAPTER 1

YOU MAY NOT SEE WHERE IT LEADS, BUT TAKE THE LEAP WITH ME

———

Happiness exists within all of us no matter who we are, what family we were born into, or what we may have done up until this point in life.

Isn't that a wild thought? The thing people most pursue in this world is already within them. What a big, ironic middle finger from the universe to human beings. Why did no one say anything? Why did no one tell you at a young age, "Hey, don't worry. That thing you want most in the world? You know, that feeling of peace and mental equanimity? It's not something you chase. Everything you will find out there is temporary, and what you're looking for exists within you."

Happiness—that sought after, more precious than gold commodity—is really based on how we think.

"Happiness does not depend on what you have or who you are, it solely relies on what you think."

—THE BUDDHA

The very words *happiness, positivity,* and *optimism* immediately conjure up different images for every person who hears them. For some, they may see a giant bank vault full of untold treasure. Others may see a beach with gentle waves lapping against their feet while they sit in a lounge chair, mai tai in hand. Some people's idea of happiness is spending time with their family and friends. Just like a fingerprint, each person's view on what makes them happy is unique to them.

My outlook on happiness, positivity, and optimism stemmed from a short time period of change and growth in my life. Throughout this time, I wanted to infuse happiness, positivity, and optimism in my life and the lives of those around me but I didn't quite know how.

During my junior year of high school, my maternal grandfather was diagnosed with dementia and later, cutaneous T-cell lymphoma. In addition, my maternal grandmother had suffered multiple strokes which set in motion a gradual cognitive decline. With my parents separating when I was young and my mom being an only child, I wanted to do everything in my power to help my mom and grandparents.

I saw the emotional toll my grandfather's disease took on my mom. Seeing those I loved in pain and struggling zapped the positivity and happiness out of me. When I left for college across the country, I worried about what would happen with my family while I was away.

From nearly three thousand miles away from home, my family was on my mind each day. I knew I had to follow my own path in college to take advantage of the educational, athletic, and professional opportunities afforded to me, but it was difficult. It tore me up inside when I would talk with my mom on the phone and she would describe her and my grandparents' struggles back home. I felt helpless being so far away.

In February of my junior year, my Uncle Michael (a close family friend who I've known since birth who was also my mom's business partner) was diagnosed with stage four prostate cancer. Because he started chemotherapy shortly after his diagnosis, my mom was forced to close their business to help take care of him.

This was hard to process on top of my grandfather's worsening disease. I knew I had to focus on baseball season, my academics, and my summer internship search, but my concern for my ailing family members stayed in my mind throughout my junior year as I received daily updates from my mom.

I felt trapped and internally conflicted. I had worked hard to achieve my dream of playing college baseball and excelling at a high academic institution, and the thought of giving up broke my heart. I had made lasting friendships with my teammates and with my classmates and was enjoying the independence of being away from home and becoming my own person in college. I was told college was supposed to be the best four years of my life, but it was difficult to relax and enjoy the time when my journey was being interrupted by external factors outside of my control.

So I did what I thought was best to take back control. After the completion of my first three years playing Division I baseball, I made the most difficult choice of my life. I consulted family and friends, and during the summer before my senior year I ultimately decided to give up college baseball and my senior year with my friends at school to come home and take care of my family.

It was painful to call each coach, teammate, and friend from school weeks before classes started to let them know I wasn't coming back.

This was made worse by having to explain my reason for leaving school over and over again to each person I spoke with. Knowing I would not be able to share the memories of my senior baseball season and my senior year with my friends was an unfortunate reality I struggled to accept. I knew I was making the right choice for my family, but it did not make it easier to walk away from my teammates and my friends at school. But I will stand by my decision for the rest of my life.

That summer we celebrated my grandfather's eighty-sixth birthday a few days after my junior year in college. He couldn't tell you it was his birthday though. He couldn't even tell you his name, and I was just another person visiting him as often as I could. His world had shrunk down to the confines of the house he had built for my mom and grandmother in the 1970s. His mind had been overtaken by his disease.

As we gathered in the kitchen, my grandfather ate his two slices of cake then turned to his presents. The first one was a pair of brown loafers—the only shoes he would wear. He took them out of the box and stared at them in amazement. We had gotten him this new pair since his old ones were worn. He undid the wrapping, lifted the lid of the box, and looked at its contents. He suddenly exclaimed with the purest form of wonderment and excitement, "Wow this is magical! This is amazing!" He kept repeating the words as he inspected the shoes.

This blew me away and changed my perspective. His disease took so much from him, yet it didn't take away his ability to positively affect others and to create happiness in those around him. He had no idea how special that moment was to everyone in the room.

I looked over and saw my mom crying tears of joy, and I took a mental snapshot of that pure moment. They were just a pair of shoes, but my grandfather looked like a kid receiving a Christmas present he's been wanting all year. His happiness spread throughout the room, and for a moment in time, I forgot about how this might be his last birthday and how the disease had taken so much from him.

Shortly after making my decision to stay home, I immediately was thrown into the real world and faced another unexpected challenge. During a routine physical, my bloodwork showed I tested positive for Hashimoto's Disease, an autoimmune disease which affects my thyroid. My thyroid levels were lower than they should be, and my doctor prescribed me a daily medication to combat it. He told me to monitor my daily energy level and keep an eye out for any changes in my mood or body.

It was another obstacle on my path, but my focus was still on my family as I entered the fall semester of my senior year of college at a university in Los Angeles.

I worked a full-time job while I took a full course load and also helped the hospice nurses and care givers with my grandfather after work multiple days a week. I slowly adjusted to my new environment, and I was driven by my love for my family and my desire to help them in any way I could.

However, as I built a routine around my responsibilities at home, I began seeing videos on social media of my teammates practicing across the country and my friends back at school having fun social lives. It was a constant reminder of what I had given up to be with my family. Instead of dwelling on what I was missing, I tried to remind myself why I made my decision to further motivate me to work for my family.

While at home helping my mom and grandparents, I noticed something. Through my grandfather's dementia, my grandmother's strokes, and my mom's medical issues, there was one thing those diseases could never permanently take away: their happiness. Of course, there were bad days, tears, and yelling, but I could always see how happy they made each other. When we sat down to eat or watched something together on TV, we focused on enjoying the moment. Our love for each other was apparent, and no disease could break that bond.

When life became difficult, as it often does in everyone's lives at one point or another, I experienced first-hand the power of positivity and optimism during a trying time. I learned silver linings really do exist, and happiness, regardless of external circumstances out of your control, exists within you.

In *The Wizard of Oz*, the Wizard tells the Tinman he had a heart all along, the Scarecrow had a brain, and the Cowardly Lion had courage the whole time. Each character had a moment of self-realization which changed their perspective on how they viewed their situation and what they desired.[6]

My grandfather's dementia took his ability to remember his own name or who his family members were, but it could never take his smile, his laugh, and his ability to light up a room. When he was confused in a conversation, he would just start spontaneously laughing, and when he said goodbye he would always leave with an "I love ya babe."

My grandmother watched the love of her life slowly decline over the years, but she resolved to enjoy every moment because she knew the disease could not take away the core of the man she married. She would always tell me stories of my grandfather and her when they were younger, and each story was always a happy memory and brought about smiles and laughter.

In listening to her stories and spending time with my grandparents, I began to think. Why would I let someone else or something else outside of my control dictate my happiness? I could not change that my family was going through a hard time because that was our reality.

---

6   *The Wizard of Oz*, directed by Victor Fleming (1939; Beverly Hills, CA: Metro-Goldwyn-Mayer).

What I could do is change the way I viewed the situation.

TAKING RESPONSIBILITY

I knew I could take responsibility for my happiness and saw how it could translate into other areas in my life. Phrases like "I will be happy if I get that car I've been saving up for," "I'm happy because I finally broke into that social circle," and "I'm happy because my favorite team scored the winning touchdown" now appeared different.

With this way of thinking, an object or a person was my source of happiness. If I took that concept a step further, it meant the object or person *controlled* my happiness. If I get that car, I would be happy. If I get into that social circle, I would be happy. If my team scores the touchdown, I would be happy.

In that moment, I felt great because my journey led to the destination of happiness, and I got what I originally wanted. It's a feeling of relief, excitement, and eagerness we love to feel.

But I thought about what happens if that car jumps in price or the people I thought were my friends exclude me... poof! The possibility of happiness is replaced by anger, sadness, regret, and all those other negative emotions no one likes feeling. The journey feels pointless because the destination was the only thing in my sights. In recognizing my ability to take responsibility for my own happiness, I found out how powerful my perspective can be. It is something to be cherished.

I have been told to chase my dreams and strive to be a good person in every aspect of my life. The very next thing I was told was: I will be happy if I accomplish my dream. I will be happy if I meet new friends or if I get that job I have wanted since I was a kid. I will be happy if I can afford to buy that beach house or if I have celebrities and athletes on my speed dial.

Because I was told this as my brain began forming at a young age, this is what my idea of happiness started off as. If I brought certain material things into my life, they would make me happy which would permeate to all other aspects of my life. When people said to find happiness, I thought it was finding those objects like a fancy car or a big house.

But I now know this isn't the case. We all learned about happiness in different ways as children, and it evolved as we got older. Now we have the opportunity to adjust our perspective and take responsibility for our happiness together on this journey.

A CHANGE IN PERSPECTIVE

Happiness is not seeing the world through rose-colored glasses and ignoring the hardships or negative events which have occurred in our lives. What if we switched out our binoculars for glasses? No, not rose-colored glasses, but normal glasses so we can adjust our perspective, which it is a great analogy for how we see happiness.

These dreams of the friends, job, house, and celebrities are part of the *binoculars' view.* This way of thinking can only be achieved in a material way and creates a tunnel-vision view of happiness like looking through the end of a pair of binoculars. Aristotle famously said, "Happiness is a quality of the soul, not a function of one's material circumstances," and he couldn't be more right.

With this view, I can *only* be happy if I get into that school, if I get that job, if I make that friend, or if I meet my definition of success. So in turn, I put the blinders on and raced toward those dreams from a young age, keeping my eye on my goals at the other end of the binoculars the whole time. But this set up a situation where I wanted to achieve my goals so badly I was willing to do anything to make it a reality.

So my happiness became predicated on my ability to accomplish that goal. I've heard the phrase "It's not the destination, it's the journey" many times throughout my life, but didn't understand it. How can I possibly be happy at all about my journey if I don't achieve my destination?

The age-old myth says we only use 10 percent of our brains, but we have only gotten about 10 percent of the happiness story while trying to achieve as close to that 100 percent as we can. It's difficult to play and win a game without knowing all of the directions.

To understand the directions, we must first recognize there is no roadmap for life, and happiness is not a Rubik's Cube we can solve with the right combination. Our perspective is a powerful tool often overlooked, and as Jimmy Buffet famously said, "It takes no more time to see the good side of life than to see the bad."

We put down the binoculars and picked up the glasses so we could change our perspective on happiness in our lives. In doing so, we are not changing what we see on the other end of the lens, instead we are simply changing how we see it.

TAKE THE LEAP

We are always able to change the way in which we view a situation. As a member of Gen Z, we didn't choose to be the "social media generation," to grow up during a period of incredible technological innovation, or to enter the job market in the midst of a global pandemic. But each of these concepts is a staple of the past, present, and future of Gen Z. We cannot change the past, but we can resolve to make the present the best it can possibly be to set up the future we want. And the first step starts now.

So as we begin our journey together, I ask you to take this leap with me and step on the cracks.

CHAPTER 2

APPEARANCES ARE DECEIVING, BUT ENERGY VAMPIRES HAVE NO SEAT ON THE ENERGY BUS

———

"Don't waste your energy on those who don't get on your bus."
—JON GORDON

When I was in high school, I remember a bus ride back to campus from a weekday baseball game. I had batted three for four with a single, two doubles, four RBIs, two stolen bases, and most importantly, we won a valuable league game. All my teammates were happy and laughing on the bus ride back. Even the coaches at the front of the bus were in a good mood.

As I sat in my window seat, I decided to pull out my phone and check social media. I scrolled through my Twitter account

APPEARANCES ARE DECEIVING, BUT ENERGY VAMPIRES HAVE NO SEAT … · 33 and on my feed. I saw another high school kid in my area had just been featured by one of the top high school sports writers in Los Angeles for his "stellar performance" that week. The day before my game, this other kid had thrown six scoreless innings and hit two home runs, leading his team to victory.

My smile immediately faded and my shoulders sagged when I read this. Compared to this other player who I didn't even know, my performance didn't seem so great anymore and I didn't feel as accomplished. While my teammates maintained their elation from our victory on the bus ride back to campus, I faked a smile and remained quiet.

When we returned to campus, I seemed to be the only one not in a good mood as we got off the bus to change in the locker room. I had been on top of the world when we were gathering our gear after the game ended an hour earlier. Now I felt like someone had punched me in the stomach. The happiness I experienced an hour before disappeared, and it was all because of seeing one Tweet.

Each of us sits in the driver's seat of our own individual energy bus with our hands on the wheel and eyes on the road. Our energy bus is a figurative manifestation of our positive energy and desired goals in our professional, social, and romantic lives, according to best-selling author and keynote speaker, Jon Gordon, in his novel *The Energy Bus: 10 Rules To Fuel Your Life, Work, and Team with Positive Energy.*[7] As the driver of our energy bus, we have the power to open the

---

7   Jon Gordon, *The Energy Bus: 10 Rules to Fuel Your Life, Work, and Team with Positive Energy* (Chichester, West Sussex: Wiley, 2015).

doors and let people on who we believe will contribute to the positive energy of our bus. These people care and want us to reach our goals.

But according to Gordon, we can also let *energy vampires* onto our bus. True to their name, these people will suck the positive energy away from our bus and try to deter us from our happiness path. They may pose as friends, but they are not on our bus for the right purpose.

Whatever the reason—and there may not just be one—energy vampires kill the engine in our bus if we allow them to stay on board.

In reading Gordon's novel, I took this analogy to heart as I began to take an introspective look at the direction of my energy bus and who I was letting on. There was one topic which came up repeatedly as I looked at who was on my bus: *social media*.

As members of Generation Z, our interactions with social media throughout our youth have been a staple of our generation. When I was younger, I made my close friends my "siblings" on Facebook, and I learned you weren't really in a relationship until it was "Facebook Official" for everyone to see. I started playing Farmville and Club Penguin because the kids at my elementary and middle schools also played.

According to a 2016 *Common Sense Media* census report, parenting expert Caroline Knorr in a nationally represented study of 1,786 parents with children ages eight to eighteen found approximately "half of kids have some sort of social media by age 12." 56 percent of those children own their own social media accounts with 80 percent of all teenagers owning their own accounts as well as 23 percent of tweens age eight to twelve.[8]

Everyone was on social media, and I quickly felt the desire to join the masses. Kids cared about the content on their social media profiles, and it was suddenly important how many followers I had, how many likes I got, and who those likes and follows came from. My social media platforms became an extension of myself and were open season to judgment from others. Every picture, every status update, every tweet, and every post were available to the scrutiny of the world.

I decided to ask some of my friends and fellow Gen Z members how they felt about social media and what role it has played in their lives.

Ryan Joseph echoed the idea of the scrutiny aspect which comes along with social media. He said, "I've been less willing to post as I've gotten older because I know I will be judged for whatever I post. It's easier to just be an observer because of how much judgment there is on social media."

Whether I cared about social media or not, I felt the need to have an online presence if I wanted to be liked and have social success. If someone I didn't know saw my Instagram or my Facebook account, I wanted them to see the best side of me: my athletic successes, my love for my family, and

---

8   "The Common Sense Census: Plugged-In Parents of Tweens and Teens, 2016: Common Sense Media," *Common Sense Media: Ratings, Reviews, and Advice,* last modified December 06, 2016, accessed August 31, 2020.

above all, my happiness. My happiness with social media was completely distilled down to the amount of likes, followers, and praise I received for my content.

Other people were determining my happiness. It was a lonely feeling comparing myself to others on social media, and I never felt "good enough." I thought if someone out there was doing something better than me I needed to try harder to reach their level.

Still, I tried to rationalize my comparison to others on social media. I told myself I was using each comparison as motivation for self-improvement. Instead, I focused on what I perceived to be my inadequacies. This came as a detriment to my happiness because no matter what I did, I did not have the "perfect life" I saw others posting about on social media every day. I had my struggles, doubts, and bad days, but I wasn't seeing posts about those topics.

My athletic, academic, and social successes seemed diminished compared to the highlight reel of others I saw on a daily basis. Because social media was everywhere, I would constantly see other people's achievements and talents which made me feel less happy and accomplished from my own. I also felt like I couldn't just quit social media. My online presence was now a part of me, and I thought taking my social media down would hurt me more than continuing to use it.

This comparison to others on social media continued for years and affected my happiness in all facets of my life as I checked social media every day. I felt I was constantly trying to figure out what I could do to appear more appealing, like the content creators who seemed to have the perfect lives and the loyal fan bases. What did people want to see from me? How can I appeal to them?

In a 2019 study conducted by the *Center for Generational Kinetics*, researchers surveyed a group of one thousand members of Gen Z in the United States. Their findings showed "95 percent of the group are on a social media app or website at least once a week, and 1/3 of Gen Z say they spend most of their time outside of work or school on social media." Additionally, the researchers found 37 percent of the Gen Z group—more than any other generation in their national study—say social media affects their happiness. Investigating further, the researchers also found 39 percent of the Gen Z group reported social media affects their self-esteem in a negative way.[9]

Professional photographer Joe Walker explained, "I think that for our generation social media has led to this constant struggle. You know, you see these people on Instagram all over the world doing crazy things and getting all this attention all the time. Then after seeing that you kind of have those same expectations for yourself on social media and you think that's what your life's should be like. But that's just not possible to do."

Later in August of 2019, *Origin*, the in-house research arm of top advertising agency *Hill Holiday*, conducted a follow-up study looking at the social media habits of one thousand

9   "Annual Gen Z Research Studies – Trends, Stats, Attitudes & More." The Center for Generational Kinetics, last modified July 24, 2020, accessed Apr. 11, 2020.

members of Gen Z. The data showed 22 percent of the Gen Z respondents felt they were "missing out" when looking at social media. Because of this, 34 percent of the Gen Z respondents in the survey actually said they're permanently quitting social media in the near future, and an additional 64 percent stated they plan on taking a break.[10]

University of Minnesota medical school student Victoria Anderson adds on by saying, "social media takes a toll on happiness, and I think people who don't use social media or who use it in a limited fashion are happier than the people who check it every day. It can mess with your emotions in a negative way."

In citing their motivations for quitting, 35 percent of the Gen Z respondents revealed they felt there was too much negativity on social media, and nearly 20 percent of respondents felt too much pressure to get attention. Over 40 percent of Gen Z members in the survey also claimed social media makes them feel anxious, sad, or depressed. This was a slight increase from the *Center for Generational Kinetics* study earlier that same year.

This data was incredibly eye opening because I didn't realize the negative affects I had felt from social media were so widespread. However, despite a significant portion of Gen Z claiming social media causes negative emotions and conditions in the *Center for Generational Kinetics* study, it still

---

10   Oliver McAteer, "Gen Z Is Quitting Social Media in Droves Because It Makes Them Unhappy, Study Finds." *Brand Knew Magazine*, last modified Mar. 14, 2018, accessed Mar. 2, 2020.

seemed like everywhere I looked, social media was there. It had a grip on our generation.

As I arrived at college, within the first few months I noticed social media was a large factor in first impressions. Frequently if my new friends and I came across a name we didn't recognize in conversation, we responded by asking, "Can I see their Instagram?" That, ironically, was our first impression of someone—a social media platform where people showed their best life.

It was clear appearances were important, and the people I saw on social media when I scrolled through posts always seemed so happy. It seemed like every time I looked through my news feed, I constantly saw pictures of awards and achievements, relationship milestones, and life-changing trips with friends to exotic locations. I wanted to be like these people.

I wanted to feel happy and to share happiness with others, but I felt social media was a Catch 22. I continued to check social media because I felt I needed to keep up, but the content would leave me with a negative feeling the majority of the time. I couldn't take it anymore.

As I navigated through the social media scene in college, I continued to think back to Jon Gordon's energy bus analogy. I wanted to make sure my energy bus was heading in the right direction with all of my supporters on board. I began to realize the difference between reality and social media.

Pictures on Instagram are far from the pictures of our everyday reality. With Facebook, Twitter, Instagram, Tik Tok, and shows like *Catfish*, it can be difficult to distinguish social media life from reality. This specifically manifests itself for me in looking at my real friends compared to *fake* friends and followers on social media.

The *fake* friend reassures me they're in my corner, but doesn't want to see my energy bus move forward. Whenever I think about this, I remember in high school talking to one of my friends who had gone to a different school. I noticed he had unfollowed me on social media, so I asked him about it. He said, "It's nothing personal. I just need to keep my followers ratio up." I also noticed this same friend would always be there to congratulate me when I had success but was nowhere to be found when I failed and needed a friend to lean on. This friend focused on what they could take from the friendship rather than what they could give. He cared more about his online following and social media reputation than he did about our friendship.

Current Division I lacrosse player Kyle McBride said, "Friend groups get smaller as you get older for a reason. Friends are the family you choose, and when you need them, they will be there for you in a way that a social media follower can't. That's the difference between a 'real' friend and a 'fake' friend."

When I gave up my senior year of college to take care of my grandfather and uncle on hospice, when I was diagnosed with my autoimmune disease, and when I felt consumed by sadness and negativity, my real friends lifted me up. They didn't shy away when life became difficult, and when I fell, they lent out their hand. They cared about me as a person, not as a social media follower, and they wanted to see me succeed.

They were the first to send flowers to my mom when my grandfather passed away, and the first to offer to cook us meals if we needed anything. My real friends are more than just friends. As Kyle says, they are family.

I understood who my real friends were on my energy bus, and I wanted to open up to them about my struggles with social media. No good was coming out of my view on social media, and I wanted to change. I shared my struggle, and they said the "comparison aspect" had diminished their self-esteem. They also recognized everyone only shows their best life on their social media accounts.

San Francisco State University baseball player Jackson Kritsch, who I played college summer baseball with, told me in high school he felt like social media was so important and it "feels like those people you see on there have the best life ever, but then you realize that's all you're seeing."

Baylor University Law School student Tristan Crowder built on this idea, saying on social media, "people are only posting their highlights. It's one big highlight reel that isn't real life."

In discussing this further, my friends and I eventually came to a resolution. We agreed social media should be about staying connected with friends and sharing memories with them. It's not about feeling bad about aspects of our lives compared to someone else. Other people getting the likes and followers have a different life. Our pictures and our posts should be for our friends and for those we care about anyway! Lafayette College graduate, Katherine Addy, sums this up well as she says, "There will always be someone doing more than you and posting about it on social media. It's never going to be perfect, so need to focus on yourself, not them."

If we focus solely on ourselves as Katherine mentioned, and post because we are passionate about the content we are sharing, then social media becomes a source of happiness rather than negativity. The comparison aspect is a toxic happiness killer, but it was stemming from our own perception of social media, not because social media inherently made us unhappy.

In talking to my friends, I was surprised to learn their focus on likes, comments, and followers negatively affected their happiness as well. They thought they were alone in that feeling. Until I echoed their views on social media, my friends didn't know anyone else was struggling with social media. Similarly, they said it was hard to tell the difference between *real* and *fake* friends on their various social media platforms. They understood it wasn't real life, and they still wanted to find a way to develop a perspective on social media just like me.

I had the opportunity to speak with Lauren Cook, author of *Sunny Side Up* and a therapist at the University of San Diego counseling center. In working with college-age members of Gen Z every day, Lauren says, "Gen Z more than any other generation values authenticity, but they don't know how to be authentic. However, they do know how to recognize when people are 'fake.'"

Cook continued on social media's effect on our perception saying, "Social media has taught us to compare our relationships, and it is hugely addictive like a slot machine in a casino.

College students' minds are still developing, and social media alters their neural wiring and changes their brain patterns."

Social media is a double-edged sword, and its cold blade can sting our confidence and slash our happiness. But as members of Gen Z, we are the "social media generation." We have grown up through its evolution, and we continue to see its place in our lives today. Social media is truly a gift if we can adopt a positive perspective and use it in a healthy way.

By changing how I viewed social media, I felt free. I was released from the need to constantly please everyone and get the most likes and followers possible. My friends showed me social media can be a great tool to use in our friendship, and I have learned how to use my posts to spread my passion and voice to others.

Our social media platforms are our individual voices. It is our opportunity to share our triumphs and fond memories with the world, not to be compared to others. It is meant to be cherished by those we care about. Our self-worth is not defined by how many followers we have or how many likes we get on a post; it is determined by how we use our voice to affect positive change. Feel comfortable in your own skin and know you don't need the validation of likes, retweets, or follows to feel like a success on social media. You need only to recognize who you are, what you stand for, and you have a variety of platforms where your voice can be heard by the world.

CHAPTER 3

SYNTHETIC HAPPINESS IS TEMPORARY, BUT JOY REMAINS AN INTERNAL CONSTANT

———

"Joy; the kind of happiness that doesn't depend on what happens."

—DAVID STEINDL-RAST

How awesome would it be to feel great all the time? Like if there was a code for happiness, we could manually punch into our brains to spread dopamine throughout our bodies and give us that *on top of the world* feeling? When we wake up and go about our day until our head hits the pillow at night, and life would be so simply wonderful. We would just be happy.... would we be joyous? Let's explore that.

Happiness and joy are often used interchangeably to describe a feeling of goodness. They are frequently spoken in the same

breath to explain the feelings from calm satisfaction to bliss-
ful gratification. They are popular qualifiers for how people
desire to live their lives. What kind of life do you want to
live? I want to live a joyous one. What do you want to be
in life? I want to be happy. They both appeared to be the
ultimate end goal.

However, I didn't know happiness and joy were different, and
I could not describe the feeling of happiness compared to a
feeling of joy. They seemed one and the same to me, just a
good feeling to experience. I did not begin to learn how to
decipher the difference until watching a 2014 interview at the
Yale Center for Faith and Culture with Matt Croasmun and
Robert Emmons, a professor of psychology at the University
of California Davis.

In the context of *Theology of Joy*, the topic of the interview,
Emmons shares a quote he believes aptly describes the difference: "happiness is an inch deep, and a mile wide, but joy is a
mile deep and a mile wide.... Joy is deeper."[11] Whereas happiness results from an external, momentary event, Emmons
explains joy comes from within ourselves and is separate
from any external event. Joy is a long-lasting inner contentment which extends through our lives once it is cultivated,
even in moments of sadness or anger.

Well, if what Emmons is saying is true, why is the phrase
pursuit of happiness so commonly used in the world today?
It's even rooted in the very founding of the United States

---

11   Echo Eston, "Theology of Joy: Robert Emmons with Matt Croasmun,"
      Daily Motion, last modified August 23, 2015, accessed May 1, 2020.

of America. Thomas Jefferson includes it in the Declaration of Independence as an unalienable right "given to all humans by their creator, and which governments are created to protect."

To break down the difference further, Emmons details the different elements of joy, saying joy is "at the top of the pyramid of positive emotions" and "possesses an aspect of transcendence." Through this transcendence, Emmons explains "joy is about connection," and this connection "is something that is beyond ourselves." Emmons goes on to say joy is a special type of happiness. In this special type of happiness, joy is cultivated through this transcendent connection "with someone else or something else outside of ourselves."

I now understood there was, in fact, a difference between happiness and joy. But, I thought about why, if joy is the more permanent state of contentment and peace, people didn't instead say "I want to be joyous." This concept was intriguing and presented a new perspective to consider on what it meant to live a happy life as I grew older.

I wanted to find a way to pursue joy and happiness and attain the inner peace Emmons discussed. It sounded amazing to be joyous and to be happy. It seemed so rare to be happy not simply because any one good thing happened, but instead because of an inner peace radiating out into the world. However, another piece of research helped show me this feeling of happiness is not something I *pursue.*

This research was conducted by Daniel Gilbert, a professor of psychology at Harvard University. Professor Gilbert is also known as "Professor Happiness" due to his work on the intersection between positivity and the human condition. One of my biggest takeaways from his research and his book, *Stumbling on Happiness,* is humans possess the capacity to experience two different kinds of happiness: natural happiness and synthetic happiness.

First, Gilbert describes natural happiness as simply being "what we get when we get what we wanted."[12] In accomplishing a goal such as acquiring a job, getting married, winning first place in a contest, or getting a *like* or *follow* on social media, that result makes us naturally happy. Gilbert adds on by saying "freedom, the ability to make up your mind and change your mind, is the friend of natural happiness, because it allows you to choose among all those delicious futures and find the one that you would most enjoy."

Mark Glover, a current medical school student at Wake Forest University, said, "When I think of natural happiness, I think of my family and my home when I was a kid. I had everything I wanted in one place with the people I cared about. And now when school or sports get difficult, I think about those times, and it just makes me happy. It was simple. And when I think about my future, that's the kind of natural happiness I want when I have a family as well."

He uses the simple example of ordering off a menu at a restaurant or an ice cream shop. We will choose the entrée or flavor we believe will make us the happiest of all the possible

---

12 Daniel Gilbert, *Stumbling on Happiness* (New York: Random House, 2007).

choices. In those moments, we *feel* happy in a comfortable and familiar environment.

The kitchen had what we wanted or the shop was in stock of our flavor of choice, and gives us a good feeling knowing things went the way we wanted them to go.

With natural happiness, the feeling things are going our way can extend to all areas of our lives. For some, it's catching the tail-end of a sports game after a long day, surfing the best wave of the day at sunset, or sledding down a hill in freshly fallen snow first thing in the morning. Each of us has external activities which bring us pleasure, and these activities all share one thing in common: they are all temporary in nature.

Differing from natural happiness, Gilbert distills synthetic happiness down to "what we make when we don't get what we wanted." Gilbert explains synthetic happiness is unique to human beings, and no other being on the planet can experience or create synthetic happiness.

This is the "happiness we create for ourselves" according to Gilbert, and it is manifested in the brain's frontal lobe. It activates our "psychological immune system" which can produce the feeling of happiness even in the event we don't actually get what we want.

Synthetic happiness is a form of personal psychological happiness which gives human beings the unique ability to still be happy even during an unhappy situation. Unlike natural happiness, freedom is the enemy of synthetic happiness.

When we have the choice between multiple options, each with a different outcome, it will cause people to agonize over "making the best decision."

In this distinction, Gilbert attempts to challenge the idea unhappiness must be the result of not getting what we want in a given situation. He also refutes the notion synthetic happiness is inferior to natural happiness. Instead he's arguing both forms of happiness are equally good however, they are manifested in different ways in our lives.

When I told Lafayette College graduate Jillian Turkmany about the difference between happiness and joy, as well as the two different forms of happiness, she said, "I think a lot of people struggle because they focus so much on their short-term happiness rather than the long-term permanence of joy. It takes so much energy for us to use synthetic happiness and to create that good feeling when we're down. People focus more on natural happiness because getting what you want is just easier. And I've always admired the people who seem like they use synthetic happiness so often because they just seem happy all the time."

In his TEDx Talk *Why We Make Bad Decisions* in 2008, Gilbert says, "there are two kinds of errors people make when trying to decide what the right thing is to do, and those are errors in estimating the odds that they're going to succeed, and errors in estimating the value of their own success."[13]

---

13 Dan Gilbert, "Why We Make Bad Decisions," *TED*, last modified July 2005, accessed Apr. 29, 2020.

As an anecdotal example, Gilbert tells the story of More-ese Bickham, a man who spent thirty-seven years in the Louisiana State Penitentiary although there was nota-ble doubt he had committed the crime of which he was accused. Upon being released at age seventy-eight for good behavior and serving half of his original sentence, Bickham said, "I don't have one minute's regret, it was a glorious experience."

Gilbert explained Bickham used synthetic happiness while in prison to create contentment for himself when the possibil-ity of natural happiness was severely diminished during his sentence. He couldn't take part in all the activities he would like to while in prison so synthetic happiness, the happiness he created for himself, was his way of coping with his unfair situation. Using his frontal lobe, Bickham realized his envi-ronmental limitations and formulated the ideal perspective for him to achieve happiness while in prison.

After speaking on the differences and impact of natural and synthetic happiness, Gilbert makes a point of noting no one can be happy all the time. He likens this idea to a compass always pointing in the same direction, thus ren-dering it meaningless. Ultimately, there can be no happy times without times of misery and strife. Those times allow us to appreciate the happy times by comparison in our lives.

Gilbert continues by saying in his 2006 TEDx Talk, *The Sur-prising Science of Happiness,* "our longings and our worries are both to some degree overblown, because we have within us the capacity to manufacture the very commodity we are constantly chasing when we choose experience."[14] That commodity is *happiness.*

In *Stumbling on Happiness* Gilbert explains human beings tend to always remember the bad times they've been through, and they oversize their future suffering by fixating on the bad times. We have a bad habit of focusing on the bad times and dwelling on them long after they have occurred. This oversizing creates a lack of trust in our ability to handle pain, which leads to further suffering and a focus on the bad times, according to Gilbert.

This concept hit home as I thought of my own trials and tribulations. Gilbert further explains confidence in ourselves and a resilience to the pain of the bad times is what gets us out of that dark place. When I realized I was causing my own pain by choosing to focus on my bad times, I felt a mix of emotions.

I was mad I had let something within in my control the whole time cause internal struggle, sad I had let myself focus on them so much, and hopeful this information could help me change my perspective. To move past the obstacles of pain and negativity, Gilbert says the first step is wanting to be happy. This seemed obvious at first, but I understood what he was saying. Tying into synthetic happiness, the choice to be happy is an active and conscious decision, not just a dream or novel idea.

---

14   Dan Gilbert, "The Surprising Science of Happiness," *TED*, last modified February 2004, accessed May 2, 2020.

Upon learning about these two forms of happiness from Daniel Gilbert, I wanted to share what I had learned with my friends. When I told him about the two different kinds of happiness, University of Virginia graduate Ezekiel Berg said, "It's always interesting to me when I think about happiness because it's so hard to define. It's just a feeling that you know, but can't really articulate. I think for me, as a kid, it was more about the natural happiness. You're just happy to play and to enjoy each day. But now as an adult, I see myself starting to use synthetic happiness more often because life gets hard, and that can help you retain that good feeling even in tough situations.

My choice of a new perspective after my family hardships was to view life as my opponent in a boxing match. I began to think of my daily successes as getting a few jabs in, maybe a body shot, and maybe even an uppercut to send Life down to the mat. Those jabs were the test I aced, the body shot was the internship I earned, and the uppercut was being able to cheer my mom up when she was upset.

In those moments, I felt like a million bucks. But inevitably Life will get back up, and the boxing match continues. Now it's Life's turn to be on the offense, and I take a few jabs off the cheek, a shot to the ribs, and a shiner on the chin which sends me onto my back. The jabs to the cheek was the parking ticket I got for being three minutes late, the rib shot is the hour-and-a-half in traffic on the way home from work, and the shiner on the chin is having to stay up late to work on an assignment.

Screenwriter and Loyola Marymount University student Trey Fearn gave me another analogy to consider and related it directly to happiness in our lives. He said, "The way I see it, our happiness in life starts off kinda like a glass house that's twenty stories high and built on Play-doh. You go through different events and sometimes it feels like your house shatters or gets knocked over. But the goal is to continue building and building until you have that strong cement foundation and a sturdier and more secure structure. I think that idea of synthetic happiness can really help that because you're able to be proactive in your building instead of reacting to what happens to you."

When my family members fell ill and my surrounding environment took on a melancholy aura, I felt a wave of negative emotions wash over me. I came across the research of Joe Dispenza and his novel *Breaking the Habit of Being Yourself: How to Lose Your Mind and Create a New One*. Dispenza says there is a refractory period when we go through trauma.

This refractory period can be as short as a few days, a *mood*, can last a few months, a *temperament*, or last years and become a *personality trait*.[15] In finding this research I realized Dispenza was echoing Daniel Gilbert and the Buddha. Happiness is based on how we think, and despite what negative event may have just occurred in our lives, we have the option to turn our refractory period into a new perspective on life.

---

15 Joe Dispenza, *Breaking the Habit of Being Yourself: How to Lose Your Mind and Create a New One,* (Carlsbad, CA: Hay House, 2016).

Dispenza points out by age thirty-five, 95 percent of who we are is a memorized set of behaviors, attitudes, perceptions, and beliefs hardwired into our unique being. I thought if I got a head start, by the time I reach thirty-five I can make sure those memorized sets of behaviors and attitudes are positive and beneficial to my life and to those around me.

I want everything in my hardwired being to encompass the drive and resolve which will keep my energy bus moving with purpose in the desired direction in my life. I saw this as part of my training in my boxing analogy. Every time I get into the ring, I can show Life I will continually rise when I'm knocked down, and I'm the one in control.

It is important for Gen Z to first understand the difference between happiness and joy, and to also realize there are multiple forms of happiness. Using this as our foundation, we can move on to how we can utilize both forms of happiness to ultimately obtain joy. But it starts between our ears before it can manifest itself in our reality.

We all go through trauma and refractory periods in our lives. These difficult times are inevitable, but our understanding of natural and synthetic happiness can help arm us with the knowledge to shorten that refractory period before it can become a personality trait. This will help us maximize our joy and minimize our pain because we can focus on creating our happiness. Our ability to affect change and leave our mark on history is directly contingent on our perspective. The first step in developing the ideal perspective is to actively and consciously want to be happy in the world we are inheriting.

CHAPTER 4

PETER PAN WANTS TO STAY A KID, BUT HE TAUGHT ME HOW TO GROW UP

———

"Life's not easy, it's not fair, it never has been, and it never will be."

—MATTHEW MCCONAUGHEY

What does it mean to be a kid? Despite every adult constantly reminding me I was one, I didn't know. University of Oklahoma graduate Connor Scanlan explained, "When you're a kid, you have few obligations and few things to stress about. Your world is just what you see around you. You have so much freedom to chase what you want before thinking about adulthood."

I was just happy to go about my day doing things I enjoyed. Misfortune and sadness were foreign concepts.

Everything appeared new and exciting, and every day was a new adventure where I was given the opportunity to feed my curiosity and explore. My life revolved around school, sports, my family, and my friends. They formed a protective bubble in my life, and the bubble was safe and comfortable.

But as I was slowly exposed to the outside world, I was introduced to all the misfortune and sadness out there. One day I saw a UNICEF commercial raising money for impoverished children in Africa, and I saw how skinny and malnourished the kids looked. This made me sad. Another day, I saw a pet adoption commercial trying to get people to donate and adopt pets so the animals wouldn't be put down. This made me cry. Another day, I went with my mom to the grocery store and saw my first homeless man holding up a sign which said, "Anything helps" and asking for spare change. This seemed unfair.

Fairness mattered a lot when I was a young kid. When something bad would happen to someone I cared about, I wondered why it hadn't happened to a bad person instead. When I saw an injustice occur in a movie, it hurt me as if I actually knew the actor on the screen. Everything was supposed to be just, and the good guys were always supposed to win. However, outside of my protective childhood bubble, *this wasn't the case in the real world.*

I turned to the adults in my life for clarity on why bad things happen to good people and why life isn't fair. However, my parents, teachers, and coaches could not give me an answer which satisfied my ever-curious young mind. No one could give me an answer solving this conceptual problem now on my mind, which bothered me.

In place of a satisfying answer, my parents told me bad things will always happen in life and not everything will go the way we expect. They explained each event, good or bad, now became part of my reality, and *I needed to accept that.*

Still, I just didn't understand. It was hard to accept a reality where I took a smiling picture with my family in an isolated moment of happiness is the same one where people cheat, lie, murder. and steal. I realized at a moment while I was happy, some other kid in a different place was sad. Every day, people get married, people have children, and people launch their career in a new job. But on those same days, someone got divorced, someone died, and someone was fired from their job. I was young, and this was a tough idea to handle.

I wanted to revert back to the innocence of childhood happiness before I learned how much sadness, despair, and unfairness is out there in the world. I wished I could be a kid forever and not have to deal with any of the negatives in life. I wanted to just live in a happy world all the time; ignorance was bliss. But as the adults told me, that wasn't reality, and I needed to grow up.

In addition to coming to terms with bad things happening to good people and life being unfair, I still struggled knowing bad things can happen every day and I did not have the power to stop them. I was told by my parents again there will always be things out of my control in life, which was something I needed to accept as I grew up. Then my parents told me I can only control what I do, so my focus should be on what I can control.

So I made it my mission to focus on what a nine-year-old could control. I ate my vegetables, drank my milk, and limited sweets to special occasions. I took academics seriously, and I played every sport offered in every season at my local park. Each night, I did my best to get my full eight-to-ten hours of sleep, and overall I just tried to be a good kid.

I gradually began to not resist growing up as much when I realized all the cool things grown-ups get to do. They don't get told what to do, they can eat whatever they want, and they don't have a bedtime. That sounded like a pretty sweet deal, and it softened the idea of leaving the comforts of childhood happiness.

This idea slowly translated into me saying "I just wanna be a grown up!" as I approached my first double-digit birthday. It usually came in response to one of my parents telling me "You're too young" or "You'll understand when you're older" to one of my requests for something. Now I was intrigued by the freedom offered by growing up, but the idea of accepting a reality where life is unfair loomed in the back of my mind.

With this new shift to wanting to be a grown up, I found it puzzling when I heard an adult say, "I wish I was younger." Now that I am older, *I understand the cyclical irony here.*

The kid wants to be an adult so badly until they realize all the responsibilities involved in being an adult, all the things which aren't advertised. The adult sees the kid playing with little responsibilities and burns with nostalgia for those times.

Associate account strategist at Google Owen Rothman said, "It's something that's been hitting me really hard lately. As I leave college, I feel like my childhood is in a sense ending. I've lived twenty-two years, and I feel like each day I've tried to be curious, have fun, and enjoy the world. Now I feel like things are rapidly getting serious, and I've tried to continue to foster that mindset remembering my childhood curiosity and happiness. If I just focus on the seriousness of being an adult, it makes me discontent because really nothing is inherently different from how it was four years ago. Yes, I have more responsibilities, but I try not to lose that mindset."

However, at ten years old I wasn't even thinking about how adults dealt with bills, taxes, and a job. I just focused on the freedom to come and go as they pleased without an authority figure telling them what to do. When I heard adults talk about having their "simpler times" back, I didn't really understand what that meant.

Two-time national champion collegiate volleyball player Caitlin Keefe said, "I always took on a lot of responsibility as a child because I wanted to be like a grown up. But as you grow up, you have to take care of yourself, and in doing so, you realize that your child-like sense of happiness never leaves you."

Continuing to ponder the idea of growing up, there were multiple movies made during my childhood and adolescence which brought the idea of a visual reality.

Freaky Friday came out in 2003 starring Lindsay Lohan as teenage rocker Anna Coleman. With Jamie Lee Curtis playing the role of Tess, Anna's mom, the movie depicts the story of how Anna and Tess's brains switch bodies after a magic fortune cookie grants each of their wishes to have the other's life. Both Anna and Tess are convinced the other's life will be easier, but Anna soon finds being an adult isn't what she thought it would be like and being a kid again isn't as easy as Tess remembered.[16]

Another movie which highlights this desire to change ages for a better quality of life is *17 Again*, which came out in 2009 and features Matthew Perry playing the role of Mike O'Donnell. Unhappy with his adult life, Mike wishes to be seventeen years old again, the peak of happiness in his life, and his wish is granted by a magic janitor at his old high school. His seventeen-year-old self, played by Zac Efron, initially enjoys the benefits of being back in high school, but he soon realizes he misses his wife, his kids, and his old life. Similar to Tess Coleman in *Freaky Friday*, Mike O'Donnell misses his adult life while being a kid and desires to return to his own age and timeline.[17]

These movies had me thinking as a kid. I used to lay in bed at night with a ton of thoughts flying around my childhood mind, and I came up with one wish. Out of my own curiosity for the future, I wished I had a time machine or a crystal ball to see what being an adult was really like.

---

16 *Freaky Friday,* directed by Mark Waters (2003; Santa Monica, CA; Walt Disney Productions).

17 *17 Again,* directed by Burr Steers (2009; Santa Monica, CA: New Line Cinema).

But at a sleepover at my friend's house when I was ten, I saw a movie called *Click* starring Adam Sandler and found even more clarity.

In the movie, Adam Sandler's character Michael Newman struggles with balancing a family life and a work life. He has a selfish and unforgiving boss who overworks him, which causes him to spend less time with his family.

One day, Michael is given a magic remote by a mysterious man after accidentally wandering into the "Way Beyond" section of Bed, Bath, and Beyond. The remote controls life, and all Michael needs to do is "point and click" to pause, slow down, and speed up life in real time.

Newman uses the remote to make his life better at work and spend more time with his family, but after working initially, the remote malfunctions and begins to control his life. The remote gets stuck on fast-forward, and Newman misses seeing his kids grow up. On his death bed, he finally gets the importance of living in the moment, and as he dies, Newman suddenly wakes up in a bed at Bed, Bath, and Beyond and realizes it was all a dream.[18]

Watching this movie as a kid showed me life is hard and sometimes unfair, but it's not meant to be controlled with a remote. If I accepted life isn't meant to be fair, I could start doing my part to make my life and lives of those around me better through my actions. The Adam Sandler comedy

---

18 *Click,* directed by Frank Coraci (2006; Los Angeles, CA: Columbia Productions).

actually showed me that instead of wishing for a time machine or crystal ball, I should focus on living my life the best way I know how.

This movie helped me, but still part of me wanted to be a kid, which stemmed from my favorite childhood movie *Peter Pan*. Peter Pan lives in Neverland, has a fairy named Tinkerbell, has a group of friends called the Lost Boys, and has a nemesis who is a pirate named Captain Hook. I loved this movie because no one aged in Neverland, and Peter Pan *never* wanted to get older.

He also has one of my favorite quotes of all time in the movie: "Keep adventuring and stay not a grown up." When I watched this movie over and over as a kid, this quote stuck in my mind, and because of it, I resolved to always stay a kid at heart no matter what happened.

Peter Pan taught me it's okay to dream, even in the darkest of times, no matter what that dream may be. He showed me even when the world feels like it's against me, I still need to maintain the faith and desire to will things to work out for the best.

I loved the movie so much I even dressed up as Peter Pan for Halloween when I was seven. I ran around my neighborhood wearing green from head to toe with a red feather sticking prominently out of my green hat.

The original story of Peter Pan actually takes place in early eighteenth century England during World War I as the Germans bombed London. When Peter Pan comes to visit Wendy and her younger brothers, they are in the most difficult time of their young lives. They do not know if a bomb will land on their house tomorrow. These children had to grow up quickly during war time, but Peter Pan helped remind them growing up doesn't mean they stop being kids at heart.[19]

When I started gaining more responsibility as I got older, the movie took on a symbolic meaning. When I had watched it as a kid, it made me want to stay a kid forever and be like Peter Pan. I was worried the wonders of childhood would fade away amongst the alarms waking me up in the morning, assignments stressing me out, and networking during a job search. However, as I grew up and gained more responsibility, I perceived Peter Pan's beliefs as "remaining a kid at heart" rather than "stay a kid forever."

Connor Scanlan added to this by saying, "My goal in life is to get where I can be a kid again. I'm working hard now to earn that freedom back that I once had as a kid. I keep that idea of childhood freedom with me always as a motivator." Like Connor, in my mind this evolution highlighted responsibility doesn't mean I needed to stop seeing the childlike joys in the world. Adulthood is inevitable, but Peter Pan showed me it does not need to be a solemn endeavor and I don't need to yearn for my youth because I will always have it within me. He showed me no matter how old I get and how much I change, I am still the child I once was on the inside if I choose to be.

---

19 Albo, Mike. "The True Story Behind Peter Pan Is Kind Of Crazy." Peter Pan True Story - JM Barrie, Davies Brothers. accessed Apr. 6, 2020. https://www.refinery29.com/en-us/2014/12/78880/peter-pan-jm-barrie-true-story.

For all of us, life can get serious very quickly. Our environments and the people around us can appear unfamiliar at times. When the unfairness of life heightens, my inner child helps me remember my perspective. I learned from Adam Sandler in *Click* life isn't fair, but that doesn't mean life is meant to be controlled for our own benefits. Peter Pan taught me to not always stay a grown up, and I used both of these movies to shape how I viewed responsibility and life's unfairness as I got older. Just because we take on more responsibility in our lives as we age does not mean we have to lose sight of our inner child. It just means we become *big kids at heart*.

CHAPTER 5

QUITTING IS EASY, BUT DELAYED GRATIFICATION IS FOR THOSE WHO PERSIST

"When faced with defeat, the easiest and most logical thing to do is to quit. That is exactly what the majority of people do."
—NAPOLEON HILL

Wait... it's logical to quit? Well, that goes counter to nearly every movie I saw growing up. In the movies, the protagonist always faced some sort of conflict and then throughout the course of the movie found a way to overcome it by its conclusion. I can understand how quitting is easy because it takes no effort to give up on something, but I couldn't wrap my head around how quitting was a logical choice.

My parents raised me to believe if I want something, I need to strive to achieve it, and if I believed in something, I need to stand up and fight for it. They taught me obstacles and challenges were inevitable in life, but I always needed to get back up no matter how many times I was knocked down. My parents said, "we don't quit, and you are not a quitter." My upbringing was so *anti-quitting* that the last word in the world I would use to describe quitting would be *logical.*

I had a hard time believing the majority of people will quit when faced with temporary defeat. Didn't they know to get back up and keep fighting? Didn't they want to keep trying? Knowing it was hard made it worth the struggle... right?

Persistence was the opposite of quitting, and I tried to make it part of my DNA as I got older. University of Oregon senior Gabe Okmin said, "I've learned to look at temporary defeat as a stepping-stone to my success and growth. I realized that my best work doesn't come right off the bat, and persistence is the path necessary to get to the goal you set out for. You just need to break through that initial feeling of failure." Quitting was the enemy to be battled against during a long night of studying, a grueling conditioning workout in the summer heat, or a weightlifting session where my body wanted to give out and fail on me.

I started looking to stories of persistence for motivation when I felt like giving up on something. I read stories about Michael Jordan being cut from his high school basketball team and working hard to climb the ladder to success. He eventually became an NBA legend through his hard work. I read about how actor Jim Carrey wrote out a ten-million-dollar check to himself in 1985 for "acting services rendered," dating it ten years into the future. He kept the check in his wallet, and despite numerous setbacks in his acting career, through his persistence, ten years later Carrey made ten million dollars for his lead role in *Dumb and Dumber* in 1995.

One of my favorite stories of temporary defeat leading to success comes from R.U. Darby, and his story is captured in Napoleon Hill's best-selling novel *Think and Grow Rich*. After accepting a challenge given to him by steel magnate Andrew Carnegie, Hill spent twenty-five years meeting and interviewing the most successful leaders of the day and compiling his studies into his book.

My former strength and conditioning coach throughout high school and early on in college, Mark Hoffman, gave me this book to read before he passed away. Not only does it hold sentimental value for me, but *Think and Grow Rich* has helped me to conceptualize my goals and work on willing them into existence through an action plan.

The week before I left for college, Mark wrote a note on August 17, 2016 on the inside cover of the book before he handed it to me. He wrote, "This book has been around for three quarters of a century, and its truths still hold solid. Pay particular attention to Chapter 15. Go be the hour big cat."

Chapter fifteen of Hill's novel is titled "How to Outwit the Six Ghosts of Fear" and covers how each of the successful business moguls Hill interviewed was able to overcome indecision, doubt, and fear on their path to success. In the chapter, Hill says, "Thought impulses begin immediately to translate themselves into their physical equivalent, whether those thoughts are voluntary or involuntary." This directly intersected with R.U. Darby's story and how temporary defeat and the prospect of quitting affect our ability to persist and find success.[20]

At the peak of the Gold Rush, Darby and his uncle traveled to Colorado in search of striking it rich, and after weeks of tireless work, they stumbled upon one of the richest gold mines in all of Colorado.

The pair continued to mine the ore in the vein, until one day it disappeared. Darby and his uncle frantically attempted to relocate the vein of gold, but *it was gone*.

They decided to cut their losses and sell their mining machinery to a junkyard. The man at the junkyard had heard about their mine and paid a mining engineer to do a calculated analysis of the area. The mining engineer discovered Darby and his uncle miscalculated their drill path and stopped *three feet short* of one of the largest gold veins in all of Colorado.

Darby and his uncle were unknowingly three feet from becoming millionaires and making history. Instead, the junkyard man achieved their dream of striking it rich in the Gold Rush.

His temporary defeat was crushing, but the young Darby decided to move on and find a job. He decided to sell life insurance, and in this decision, he turned his "quitability" into "stickability" in his new career.

---

20   Napoleon Hill, *Think and Grow Rich* (London: Penguin Group, 2005).

After quitting his mission for gold, Darby could have made quitting a habit, his "quitability," when faced with temporary defeat. Instead, he remained determined to find success, his "stickability," in his mission for selling life insurance. Where he initially sought immediate gratification in the Gold Rush, Darby persisted to find the benefits of delayed gratification in his new job selling life insurance.

He developed his life motto: "I stopped three feet from gold, but I will never stop because men say 'no' when I ask them to buy insurance." He refused to make quitting a habit, and in doing so, he became one of the most successful life insurance agents of the late nineteenth and early twentieth century, recouping his losses from the Colorado mine many times over.

Darby chose to be success conscious and used his defeat in the Colorado mine to fuel his success as a life insurance agent. He recognized his failure but saw through patience and persistence, delayed gratification was possible.

This idea of persistence intrigued me, and I dove into my research to learn more. I came across the research of Angela Duckworth, a professor of psychology at the University of Pennsylvania, who is considered to be the world's leading expert on *grit*. Duckworth defines *grit* as a sustained persistence and passion directed toward a long-term goal, with no focus on any accolades or recognition to be achieved during the pursuit. According to Duckworth, *grit* is the biggest predictor in an individual's potential success in a given endeavor.

Beginning in 2007, Duckworth and a team of researchers conducted a study of 11,258 West Point cadets over a period of ten years on the cadets' cognitive ability, physical ability, and grit from their entry into West Point to graduation.

The study began during the "Beast Barracks," which is a famously difficult six-week training program to start a cadet's West Point career. Duckworth and her team had tracked the student's cognitive and physical abilities through tests, and to measure grit they administered a twelve-point "grit scale" evaluation to the cadets who successfully completed the "Beast Barracks." This twelve-point test would determine each cadets' capacity for perseverance.

Of the 81 percent of cadets who graduated from the initial group, Duckworth and her team found "grit" was the most important factor in their success.[21] Additionally, Duckworth and her team found although cognitive and physical abilities helped enable the cadets to progress forward in their training, their *grit* allowed them to continue on during the toughest times of their training.

After talking with Sidney, I thought back on phrases I had heard from my parents growing up when I experienced temporary defeat. These phrases included "everyone makes mistakes" and "don't worry you'll get 'em next time." But, following those phrases my dad would ask me, "So, are you going to let this define you?"

---

21   Jorge Fitz-Gibbon, "'Grit' More Important to Success than Brains and Brawn, West Point Study Finds," *New York Post,* November 04, 2019.

He has asked me this question many times in my life, but I specifically remember him saying them while I was crying on the way home from the last soccer game I ever played. My club team consisted of my childhood friends, and we had played together for years. We knew with everyone going to different high schools, this was our last year together. For most of us, it was our last year playing soccer.

We had advanced to state finals, and after a hotly contested regulation time and overtime, the score was 0–0, and we went into penalty kicks.

I was chosen by my coach to take a penalty kick for our team. In my last moment of competitive soccer with my teammates and parents watching me, I directed my kick at the bottom left-hand portion of the goal. The goalie guessed correctly and blocked the ball. We lost in penalty kicks, and my last kick in a soccer game was forever going to be that moment.

I cried with my friends, knowing our time together as teammates had ended. I had an opportunity to help my team, and I failed. I could feel the memory slowly being burned into my brain as I walked to the car with my dad.

He could obviously see I was upset, and he stayed silent for a while before asking me, "Are you going to let this define you?" He said, "You missed, and it's over. It's a game. You can't change that it happened, but you can control what you do now."

My dad helped me see my temporary defeats could only define me if I let them. I had the choice of whether I would give up or persist and turn temporary defeat into success. I could've been failure conscious of what I failed to accomplish, but I wanted to be success conscious like R.U. Darby. My dad, in connection with this idea, told me delayed gratification would lead to success to those who persisted.

In further looking at delayed gratification, the famous Stanford Marshmallow Experiment was a study conducted in 1972 by Walter Mischel, a psychology professor at Stanford University. This study was repeated multiple times in various decades, the most recent study taking place in 2018. In the study, a group of children ages three to five were taken one by one into a room where the researcher offered them a choice.

The researcher laid a marshmallow in front of the child and told them if they waited to eat the marshmallow until the researcher came back, they could have two marshmallows. The researcher would then leave the room for fifteen to twenty minutes and observe the child's mannerisms. If the child successfully waited for the researcher to return, the child would receive two marshmallows as a reward for their self-control.

Mischel and his colleagues in the original study and in subsequent studies of the experiment found, contradictory to their hypotheses, the majority of the children used delayed gratification to wait for the double marshmallow reward. The children were able to endure the fifteen to twenty minutes the researcher was gone. The researchers followed these children as they grew up and found the children who used delayed gratification in the experiment had more academic and professional success as adults than the children who chose immediate gratification.[22]

Georgetown University graduate and author of *Next Gen Leadership*, Hunter Tiedemann, continued on this same idea saying that as he grew up, he would base his self-worth on immediate gratification in the form of getting good grades and doing well in sports. When he didn't get immediate gratification, he felt down, and I could relate. However, he says he hit a point where he wanted to change.

Hunter said, "I realized that you have to forgive yourself, not chastise yourself, when you make a mistake. It's not leading you astray from your path; it's a necessary part of finding the best version of you out there. Be the person your young self would be proud of."

Thomas Alva Edison personifies persistence and the patience to accept delayed gratification. Known as the inventor of the lightbulb and the telegraph, Edison often carries the title of "the greatest inventor in history." His failures in creating a successful lightbulb are well documented in history.

During his many setbacks in the process of inventing the lightbulb, Edison said, "I have not failed. I've just found 10,000 ways that won't work."

He saw each of his failures as a step closer to his ultimate goal rather than a step backward. If Edison had stopped at attempt

---

22 "The Stanford Marshmallow Experiment: How Self-Control Affects Your Success in Life," *Effectiviology,* accessed Mar. 8, 2020.

number 9,999, he would not be a household name today for his groundbreaking discovery of the lightbulb.

But how does Edison's resilience apply to Gen Z?

A 2018 survey by a New York based marketing agency, *Rhodel,* showed over 60 percent of Gen Z "want to change the world." Respondents wanted to solve world hunger, cure cancer, and end global homelessness among other dreams.[23]

These are lofty goals and amazing dreams. They will not be given to us. There will be temporary defeat on our path to accomplishing these goals and making this world better for the next generation to inherit it.

Each setback and temporary defeat in our quest to positively affect the world is a stepping-stone to our overall success. Failure loves to trip us up and make us feel like we're not good enough. Quitting is the easy way out, and it is logical. The path to success is paved with broken cobblestones and shattered glass. We may trip and fall, we may not want to continue on our path, but if we truly see the delayed gratification in our journey and we learn from our temporary defeats, we'll find success. We will rise above those who quit and get to where we want to be. In doing so, our failures will help us grow, not tear us down, and our successes will become possible because of our persistence and grit.

---

23   Rhodel Kaba, "Here's What You Need to Know About Generation Z," The Digital Strategy & Marketing Blog (blog), *Rhodel.com,* June 26, 2014.

CHAPTER 6

SHE MAY NOT HAVE HER SIGHT, BUT SHE HELPED ME SEE

——

"I want people to understand that there's never a situation too dark for you to get out of. There is always hope inside of you, and you have the power to find it."

—MOLLY BURKE

Molly Burke is one of my heroes, and I wanted to share in this chapter the positive impact she had on my life. Molly is a twenty-six-year-old from Ontario, Canada, and she is truly the embodiment of what it means to be a positive and impactful human being. Molly's story has reached millions, and her message rings true for all of Gen Z.

In hearing Molly's story for the first time, I experienced a rush of raw emotions, and it helped give me strength to push through my own dark times in life. She has helped me understand how I can incorporate positivity into my own life and the lives of those around me through the power of perspective. The world needs more people like Molly Burke.

I first came across Molly's story while researching how to find happiness and regain a positive perspective. My grandfather had just passed away from dementia, and my Uncle Michael had recently been put into hospice care with stage four cancer. I was constantly reminded I was no longer playing baseball at school, and I would never have the senior year I had envisioned with my friends.

I worked and attended school full time while helping take care of my family, and I felt my happiness getting lost in the mix of my daily responsibilities. My movements felt robotic, and I was constantly emotionally drained.

At 2:00 a.m. one night in March, I couldn't sleep. Instead, I was researching how to be happy, meticulously combing through articles on the internet to find something I could apply to my life.

In between online studies, a headline caught my eye. It read "Blind and Bullied: She Lost Her Sight and Then Things Got Worse" by Sydney Loney. The article was for *Chatelaine*, Canada's premier women's lifestyle brand, and it showed a picture of a young girl above the heading. Scrolling down slightly, the subtitle hooked me into reading the piece: "After losing her vision, Molly Burke found herself in an even darker place. Now she's giving hope to anyone who's ever felt victimized— and showing them how to fight back."[24]

---

24 Sydney Loney, "Blind and Bullied: Teenage Activist Molly Burke Shares Her Inspirational Story," *Chatelaine*, January 18, 2017, accessed Mar. 9, 2020.

Loney begins by sharing Molly was diagnosed at age four-and-a-half with *retinitis pigmentosa*, a rare, degenerative eye disease, and she lost her sight completely at age fourteen. Beginning in eighth grade, Molly was severely bullied by her classmates and fell into a deep depression, cutting her arms to feel physical pain instead of the burden of emotional pain.

She said, "I felt so alone and sad. I just wanted not to exist." Around this time, her father discovered searches for "how to kill yourself" on Molly's computer and decided Molly needed to be put in a school for the blind.

Molly was also bullied at her new school, but instead of reverting back to her depression, Molly did something amazing. She came to the realization she wasn't bullied because she was different; the other kids at the school were also blind. Molly said, "There's no reason. It's not my haircut, or how I dress, it's just something in the other person, and they've decided to target me."

Instead of feeling sorry for herself, Molly made the choice to take action. She said, "I've been through this; I've heard these things before, and the first time I ran. This time, I need to deal with it.'"

She embraced who she was and began to make new friends at her new school with her positive attitude, but the bullying continued. While walking down the hall with her mother one day, a group of kids pushed a container of ketchup and fries into Molly's path. They then jeered, "Hey, blind girl, watch where you're going!" when Molly stepped on it.

Molly's mother was enraged, but Molly told her, "It's fine, Mom. This is what I deal with. But it's okay. I have friends. I have confidence. I believe in myself and I know I'm going somewhere in life." Through everything she went through, Molly focused again on what she could control, and she understood her voice is powerful.

Molly personified Psychology Professor Daniel Gilbert's idea of synthetic happiness. In the midst of the negativity in her life, Molly created her own happiness by courageously standing up to her bullies. She used her psychological immune system to turn her negative situation into a positive one.

Molly Burke is so unique because she is not just an anti-bullying speaker working to help victims of bullying. Her message is focused toward all Gen Zers, hitting on important issues that affect young members of the generation, bullies and victims of bullying included.

In addition to Molly Burke, my friend Sophie Pollack has been an inspiration and helped me work to build a positive perspective in my life. When she was thirteen years old, Sophie was drugged and raped at a party. After spending years silent, Sophie opened up about the attack in her junior year of high school.

After opening up about being sexually assaulted, Sophie was bullied by her classmates at her high school. During this time as well, Sophie was also in an abusive relationship with her ex-boyfriend.

One of her friends approached her during her junior year and asked to do a documentary on her experience as a sexual assault survivor. Although she was nervous to share her story with the world, Sophie agreed to do the documentary with her friend.

The two friends submitted the documentary to the Archer Film Festival, and out of over seven thousand submissions, their documentary placed twelfth. Sophie said, "this was the first time the public was hearing my story and the first time I really found my voice. It was life changing."

After the documentary, people started coming to Sophie for advice in their own struggles. Amidst the bullying, Sophie was able to find the courage to speak out and brush off her bullies' jeers. She said, "I made the decision to not let the bullying affect me, and I wanted to remove their toxic negativity from my life."

Sophie then developed her foundation, A Path 2 Courage, to further her voice and be an advocate for those affected by sexual assault and domestic abuse. When she did this, she found the unconditional love and support of her family and friends and knew she wanted to help as many other survivors as possible.

She said, "I wanted to be able to change others mindsets as well. It is a sad and traumatic event to be sexually assaulted, but I wanted to show other girls that they can still be happy."

Similar to Molly Burke, Sophie also used Professor Gilbert's concept of synthetic happiness to return happiness to her life after being raped. She stood up to her bullies and changed her perspective on her situation to bring herself out of a dark place and into the light.

In doing so, Sophie used her new perspective to help others in her situation by spreading her message of positivity. She told me, "It's all about what you let get to you and what you choose to brush off. It is a sad and traumatic event to go through a sexual assault, but there is a light at the end of the tunnel for all of us." Sophie and Molly have both inspired me to use my voice to help others as well, and their stand against bullying is a model for everyone within the Gen Z generation.

Bullying is an important issue for Gen Z. A 2019 study commissioned by the Boy Scouts of America used a youth survey and the results ranked bullying the top concern for young people on a community, national, and global level.

Thirty percent of the young children in the survey said bullying was one of the problems they most wanted to solve across the globe, and 32 percent said it was the biggest issue in the US today.[25] On a local level, Gen Z youth ranked bullying higher than both hunger and caring for the elderly as topics needing the most attention to help improve their community.

Amidst the pressures to achieve at a young age to be successful later in life, and now with technological advancement, bullying has moved to cyber space as well. Additionally, the National Crime Prevention Council found in their 2014

---

25 "Bullying is Gen Z's #1 Concern According to New BSA Survey," *Scouting Newsroom* (blog), Boy Scouts of America, September 17, 2019. accessed Mar. 22, 2020.

statistics, 43 percent of Gen Z members reported being victims of cyber bullying.[26]

University of California-Berkeley graduate Chris Novia said, "I've noticed many examples of cyber bullying as I've gotten older. With social media, people create fake accounts and try to harass their victims, and it's sad. We're the first generation to really experience bullying through a computer screen."

For Gen Z, bullying has expanded from in-person abuse to online messaging where the bully can hide behind a screen pseudonym. The ease at which bullying has been able to occur in Gen Z reflects the *American Psychological Association*'s 2018 Harris Poll survey, which shows Gen Z has the worst mental health of any generation, starting from a young age.[27]

Both Sophie Pollack and Molly Burke show the Gen Z youth that each of us is in control of our own life. Just like Molly and Sophie took control of their lives and overcame their bullies, Gen Z youth can too. Their message of changing our perspective to a positivity and a comfortability with who we are in our own skin is exactly what Gen Z youth need right now.

Molly and Sophie's stories have touched so many hearts, and they have touched mine as well.

---

26 Brian Mastroianni, "How Generation Z is Changing the Tech World," CBS News, Mar. 10, 2016, accessed Apr. 21, 2020.

27 "APA Stress in America™ Survey: Generation Z Stressed About Issues in the News but Least Likely to Vote," American Psychological Association, October 30, 2018, accessed Mar. 19, 2020.

Their stories are ones of triumph and overcoming adversity, but they are also stories of bringing light to a dark situation. Molly and Sophie did exactly what Daniel Gilbert explains through synthetic happiness: they created their own happiness. In addition, they recognized they have the ability to positively affect so many with their voices. They have inspired me to recognize the positives in my own life and bring that positivity to those around me. Their unrelenting positive attitudes serve to remind Gen Z we are stronger than the negative bullies in our lives, and they help us to continue to strive for self-improvement and positivity every day.

CHAPTER 7

THE DAY MAY BE LONG, BUT I START BY MAKING MY BED

———

"If you want to change the world, start off by making your bed. If you make your bed every morning, you will have accomplished the first task of the day."

—ADMIRAL WILLIAM HARRY MCRAVEN

Make my bed? Was he kidding? I was confused how making my bed would translate into my impact on the world. When I thought of making my bed, it reminded me of my mom nagging me as a young kid to make my bed and clean my messy room. I had always thought of making my bed as a chore like taking the trash out, and I looked forward to becoming an adult and not having to do it anymore. Adults didn't really care about making their beds, right?

But at this same time, this was coming from Admiral William McRaven, a four-star Admiral, Navy SEAL, and the ninth commander of the US Special Operations Command. Outside of his military accomplishments and public speaking abilities, Admiral McRaven is also the best-selling author of *Make Your Bed: Little Things That Can Change Your Life… And Maybe the World.*

Even though I couldn't understand why he was saying making my bed was important, I was intrigued by this idea, and coincidentally I was also looking to create a morning routine or ritual to start my day.

My morning routine consisted of turning over when my alarm went off, grabbing my phone, and immediately reading texts and emails that had come in overnight. I would then scroll through my social media accounts and my daily news apps to catch up on the new content I missed while I was asleep. After feeling caught up, I would get out of bed and start my day. Actively making my bed in the morning was not even a thought.

I wasn't alone in incorporating my cellphone in my morning routine. Loyola University of Chicago graduate Penny Walsh said, "I know I'm not supposed to do it, but first thing I used to do in the morning is roll over and reach for my phone. I would scroll through social media and answer texts and emails before I left my bed, but I've really tried lately to create a morning routine that doesn't involve that. Now I try to make sure that my morning routine is productive, and spending that time on my phone in bed wasn't productive."

A 2019 study conducted by technological innovator Mobile Posse and Phoenix Marketing International "found that the race to win consumer mobile attention begins first thing in the morning when users are often times checking their devices before they get out of bed and have no particular app in mind." The data specifically showed Gen Z is more likely than any other generation to check their phone as their first act after waking up in the morning.

In fact, according to the study "65 percent of Gen Z users check their phones while they are still in bed, and 9 out of 10 of Gen Z users will check their phones before they leave their bedrooms in the morning."[28] This is significantly higher than the next closest generation. In citing the reason for checking their phones first thing in the morning, 77.5 percent of the Gen Z users in the study "want to start their day connecting with friends." This is in stark contrast to Baby Boomers, only 38.4 percent of which check their phones first thing in the morning according to the study.

So, when I heard the first of Admiral McRaven's ten lessons he learned during basic SEAL training was "Make your bed," I was skeptical.

Elaborating on his first lesson in a 2014 commencement speech to his alma mater, University of Texas at Austin, Admiral McRaven says, "if you make your bed every morning, you will have accomplished the first task of the day. It will give you a small sense of pride, and it will encourage you to do another task... By the end of the day

---

28   Robert Williams, "Gen Z Prefers Entertainment, Social Media in Early Dayparts," *Mobile Marketer*, November 22, 2019, accessed May 16, 2020.

that one task completed will have turned into many tasks completed."[29]

Admiral McRaven explains making our bed will remind us the little things in our lives matter. If we want to be able to do the big things and accomplish our goals, we have to be able to do the little things right.

He continues by saying when we've had a bad day, we can come home to an already made bed. It's a bed we made. This made bed will encourage us tomorrow will be better than today. Admiral McRaven powerfully says in front of the new University of Texas at Austin graduates, "So if you want to change the world, start off by making your bed."

I decided to try to create my own morning routine by making my bed, and it seemed like a morning chore. However, as I slowly got used to it, eventually it became a habit. Just as Admiral McRaven described, I did feel accomplished and fulfilled, and making my bed gave me a sounder morning routine as well.

I am starting my day off with a small victory. I have my first win before the race even starts. Taking pride in making my bed in the morning set me up to take pride in every action I undertake throughout the day.

I didn't even realize some of my friends had also recently tried to make the same change of starting their day by

---

29 "Adm. McRaven Urges Graduates to Find Courage to Change the World," *UT News*, The University of Texas at Austin, May 16, 2014, accessed Mar. 21, 2020.

making their bed. Current baseball player at Gonzaga University Riley Livingston said, "The premise of baseball is to get home, and I think that's a metaphor for life as well. I wanted to maximize my productivity throughout my day, and that starts in the morning with me making my bed. It's about doing the little things right and having an attention to detail."

Admiral McRaven's first lesson and its implementation in my life spurred me into reading additional research on how to minimize stress and maximize happiness in my day.

The American Psychological Association conducted their annual stress report in 2018 with 3,458 respondents and found over 91 percent of Gen Z respondents reported feeling the effects of emotional or physical symptoms of stress including depression and anxiety. At just over nine out of every ten members reporting being stressed, Gen Z scored the most stressed as well as the poorest overall mental health of any other generation.[30] The buildup of micro stress doses accumulating throughout our days as we try to achieve our ambitious goals during our transition to the professional world is one major source of this stress.

In my research, I became fascinated by Dr. Rangan Chatterjee, a general practitioner from the Edinburg University School of Medicine whose research touches on how we start our day and the effect it has on our lives. Dr. Chatterjee

---

30   "APA Stress in America™ Survey: Generation Z Stressed About Issues in the News but Least Likely to Vote," American Psychological Association, October 30, 2018, accessed Mar. 19, 2020.

focuses his research on the causes and solutions for the daily stress in our lives.

Dr. Chatterjee studies our body's response to stress. When we feel stressed, our bodies produce cortisol, which is the physical manifestation of stress in our bodies. According to Dr. Chatterjee, "stress affects every single organ in our body because actually the stress response is designed to keep us safe."

The more stressed we become, the more cortisol is released into our bodies. Cortisol also decreases the level of dopamine, one of the *feel good* chemicals in our bodies, which then decreases our feelings of well-being and happiness. Ohio State University graduate Dylan Murphy said, "When you have a lot going on, it's only natural that stress will be present in some form in your life. But the level of stress is crucial. By mitigating it to a minimum, we can function at our optimal level, and that starts when we wake up."

Dr. Chatterjee also discusses how important sleep is to the healing of our bodies and recharging of our brains. His research focuses on a wide variety of aspects of human wellness, but one piece of research stood out in connection with Admiral McRaven's first lesson.

Dr. Chatterjee identifies "micro stress doses" in our lives. These are little, tiny events that occur and in turn create "micro doses" of stress within our bodies. We may not even realize these events in the moment, but Dr. Chatterjee maintains we can gather up to ten to fifteen micro doses of stress before we even leave our house in the morning. This means we had ten to fifteen different stressors occur in the very beginning of our day from the time we wake up until the time we leave the house.

According to Dr. Chatterjee, "The more Micro Stress Doses (MSDs) you take on, the more your rational brain will be deskilled, while your emotional brain will grow ever stronger." Our alarm goes off on our phone or alarm clock in the morning, and this jolts us from our deep sleep and creates the first micro stress dose.[31]

Depending on how the previous night has gone, many people will hit the snooze button on their phone. After hitting the snooze button, a few minutes later our alarm goes off again, creating the second micro stress dose. Then after waking up from the second alarm, the next thing many of us will do is look at our phones to see all the texts, emails, and social media notifications we missed, creating the third micro stress dose. Following checking our texts and emails, Dr. Chatterjee says, "then a notification for paying bills pops up, and that creates micro stress dose #4 even before leaving your bed."

With enough of a buildup, the micro stress doses will cause us to hit our personal stress threshold in which we feel stressed and anxious. This in turn, according to Dr. Chatterjee, negatively affects our emotional state and hampers our ability to achieve our goals throughout the day.

---

31   Rangan Chatterjee, *Stress Solution: The 4 Steps to Reset Your Body, Mind, Relationships and Purpose* (London: Penguin Books, 2019).

Dr. Chatterjee's research conceptualizes why Admiral McRaven's first lesson of making our beds is important for the success of Gen Z. In the midst of micro stress doses, something as simple as making our bed can help us limit stress and promote productivity because of the sense of accomplishment it provides our psyche at the start of the day. It is amazing how folding my sheets around the corners and resetting my pillows, which takes all of thirty seconds, can make a notable difference in my day.

Former Division I college baseball player Brett Kreyer said, "Having a morning routine is the foundation for having a productive day. I do whatever I can at the beginning of my day to minimize stress, and feeling comfortable at the very start of your day after you wake up is the first step. You want to be as calm as possible leaving the house and heading into work if you want to maximize productivity and limit stress."

Admiral McRaven's lessons on mental strength and fortitude, as well as Dr. Chatterjee's research on micro doses of stress, have helped me combat and minimize the stressors in my life. These stressors of entering the real world and being successful are the *energy vampires* Jon Gordon writes about in his book *The Energy Bus.* This stress wants to suck the life out of our day from the very start. It wants to replace our endorphins and happiness with cortisol.

Stress and the presence of cortisol in our bodies can lead to acne, headaches, and insomnia according *The Mayo Clinic.*[32]

---

32   "Stress Symptoms: Effects on Your Body and Behavior," Mayo Clinic, Apr. 04, 2019, accessed May 22, 2020.

Additionally, when left unchecked for long periods of time, stress can cause mental health issues such as depression, as well as cardiovascular disease and gastrointestinal disorders.

Research done by Sheldon Cohen at Carnegie Mellon University has found prolonged psychological stress affects the body's ability to regulate its inflammatory response. Cohen's research, which was published in the *Proceedings of the National Academy of Sciences*, illustrates how by affecting the regulation of the body's inflammation response, chronic stress can promote the development and progression of disease. The hormone cortisol is used in part to regulate inflammation in the body, but when cortisol is not allowed to properly serve this function, inflammation can increase to harmful amounts. Through prolonged stress, the body is unable to effectively use cortisol to regulate its inflammatory response "because it decreases tissue sensitivity to the hormone.[33]

Ohio State University graduate Dylan Murphy said, "When you have a lot going on, it's only natural that stress will be present in some form in your life. But the level of stress is crucial. By mitigating it to a minimum, we can function at our optimal level, and that starts when we wake up."

Armed with this knowledge from Admiral McRaven and Dr. Rangan Chatterjee, I started my day by making my bed and actively seeking to maximize productivity and minimize stress. But after a long night of studying or waking up for an early workout, it was hard to get out of bed when my phone

---

33 "Stress on Disease," Carnegie Mellon University, accessed Mar. 14, 2020.

alarm blared in my ear and stole my peaceful rest away. In that moment, there is the choice of hopping up and starting the day or hitting the big snooze button.

It would be so easy to hit the snooze button. Just for five more minutes.... or ten... or fifteen. It would be so nice to drift back to peace and delay the challenges of the day just a little longer.

But snoozing the alarm comes at a cost. Time has to come from somewhere, and it gets stolen from the potential productivity of the day. It is a sign getting out of bed and starting the day isn't the priority, but five more minutes of sleep is. That's not a recipe for success; it's a recipe for future stress and bad habits.

So, I found something to help me get out of bed every morning and start straightening out my sheets once I was up. In her award-winning book and TEDx Talk, Mel Robbins discusses the five second rule on getting out of bed in the morning. She says after our alarm goes off and we become aware of our surroundings, we should countdown from five to one, then launch ourselves out of bed in the morning *like a NASA rocket ship*. Robbins says, "The countdown pushes you out of autopilot, and when you act, you're exercising control and you're turning on your prefrontal cortex."[34] Thus, our desire to snooze the alarm and delay our productivity is quelled, and we are up and ready for the day.

---

34   Mel Robbins, "The 5 Second Rule," *Mel Robbins* (blog), December 13, 2018, accessed May 7, 2020.

As we go about our morning, stressors can build on each other and multiply quickly. They present obstacles to our happiness and positivity as they attempt to deter us from taking meaningful steps toward our daily goals. But these stressors can only affect us if we let them. It is up to each of us whether these stressors will negatively impact us or if we use a morning routine to effectively combat them. We have that choice. By being cognizant of how these stressors work in our lives, we can improve our attention to detail and intention in each action at the start of our day.

Every action we take, down to the most insignificant detail, must be deliberate and intentional if we want to affect change. Making our bed is the start, and it is something to take pride in. Life gets busy, and when external career and social pressures build, it is the most important time to start the day with a victory. A positive and triumphant mindset at the start of our day prepares us to take on the world as we leave the house, and this staple of our morning routine will help give Gen Z the best chance to make the kind of impact we want to on this world.

CHAPTER 8

WORK ISN'T ALWAYS FUN, BUT I'M A GOLDEN RETRIEVER

——

"To live your life where you love Friday night, Saturdays and Sunday, but despise Monday through Thursday is devastating to me because you're wasting too much of your life"

—GARY VAYNERCHUK

"TGIF: Thank God it's Friday" and "I hate Mondays." These two days are more than just two days of the week; they are symbols of societal emotions during a work week. They are printed on T-shirts, coffee mugs, and have even been the titles of movies. Friday is the last day of the work week, and the beginning of the weekend, so the "TGIF" phrase has become popularized (even into the name of a restaurant) with a positive connotation. In contrast, Monday morning signifies the end of the weekend and the beginning of a new work week, carrying a negative connotation as well as scientific data proving more cardiovascular issues arise on Mondays.

A 2017 study conducted in Sweden by Claes Held, MD, PhD and his colleagues at Uppsala University and Umeå University and published in the *American Heart Journal* analyzed data from over 156,000 hospital admissions for a heart attack over a seven-year period. Their results showed the most heart attacks occurred on Mondays with the risk of heart attack being 11 percent higher on Mondays than any other weekday. Additionally, for young, working people, Held and his colleagues found they were most vulnerable to the Monday increase in heart attacks with their risk being 20 percent higher on that day of their workweek.[35]

These were such commonly used terms I didn't think twice about them as a kid. It just seemed I would get excited for the school week to be over and the weekend to start on Friday and going back to school on Monday wasn't fun. University of California, Berkeley graduate Allison Gist echoed this by saying, "When you're in school, it's always a countdown to the Friday afternoon because that's when you get a break from the work. So you end up looking forward to that weekend time starting at a young age." I thought this was just normal for everyone.

But as I got to high school, I was introduced to a new perspective on the school/work week. In his podcast, *The Gary Vee Auto Experience*, Gary Vaynerchuk is known around

35 European Society of Cardiology, "Global Study Sheds Light on Role of Exercise, Cars and Televisions on the Risk of Heart Attacks," *ScienceDaily*, January 11, 2012, accessed Apr. 19, 2020.

the world for his fiery messages of motivation and passion. A five-time *New York Times* best-selling author and serial entrepreneur, Gary Vaynerchuk shared one particular message that stuck with me when I first heard it in high school. The video is titled "Why Do You Hate 64.28 percent of your life?" and focuses on why so many people don't enjoy their professional careers Monday through Friday and solely live for the weekend.

This is one of my greatest fears in life: I will fall into the same unhappiness with my professional career. But Vaynerchuk believes that shouldn't be the case. Vaynerchuk says he feels sorry for the "weekend warriors" who live their lives for the weekend and dread working Monday through Friday. Instead, he uses an interesting analogy to help him look forward to the upcoming workweek. Vaynerchuk says, "Sunday night I'm like a fighter before a fight in the dressing room. I try to go to sleep early on Sunday because I can't wait for Monday because I get to put my jersey on."[36]

This line struck a chord with me, and I wanted to have a similar intensity in my professional career. I wanted to enjoy the work I am doing Monday through Friday, and I didn't want to just live for the weekend. I want this so badly because this is a concept I have battled in school. Where Gary Vaynerchuk describes himself as a fighter in the dressing room itching to get out to the fight, I felt like I was already in the fight and I was taking more punches than I was dishing out.

---

36 Gary Vaynerchuk, "Business Tips: Why You Hate 64.28% of Your Life/ A Gary Vaynerchuk Original," *Biz Channel Review Guide*, December 19, 2019, accessed Mar. 29, 2020.

I saw Monday through Friday as something to take pride in getting through and reaching the weekend. The weekend was my escape. When I heard Gary Vaynerchuk's message, I realized I was part of the group that disliked the 64.28 percent. I was focused on exceeding expectations, handling responsibilities, and beating the pressure in school, sports, and social life, but Vaynerchuk made me realize something was missing. Baylor University baseball player Daniel Caruso said, "Growing up I would see a lot of people doing a nine to five job they just weren't happy with. They did it for the money. I really value enjoying my work, and I want to find a way to make that Monday through Friday time worthwhile." The missing piece was the hunger and joy in the Monday through Friday grind he describes.

As I made the transition from high school to college, I held Gary Vaynerchuk's message in mind and attempted to change my thinking. It came down to attitude and perspective. I wasn't going to change the fact I would have parts of my Monday through Friday I didn't enjoy, but I could control how I attacked them. But as I began my freshman year of college, that idea faded, and I reverted back to being the captain in choppy waters each week.

During the summer break between my freshman and sophomore year of college, an "aha moment" came. I had gone out to dinner with a group of friends and while waiting for our food, one of my friends asked the group, "what kind of animal would you be based on your personality?"

Around the table people gave their answers and explanation, but when it got to me, even though I had thought about it,

I wasn't sure what to say. As I paused, one of my friends said, "oh, you're definitely a golden retriever." I laughed and asked her why she was so sure, and she said, "Because you have so much energy and you want to do stuff all the time." It was one of the best compliments I've ever received and made me realize it was all about perception. My friend perceived me as a golden retriever because of my actions.

On the way home, I thought about this idea. My energy and zest for life was like a golden retriever's, but in my happiness, there was a disconnect. For dogs, every day is a new adventure, but I struggled with having my daily work be an adventure. I wanted to be Indiana Jones in an archeological dig at the Temple of Doom on Monday, Inspector Jacques Clouseau searching for the Pink Panther on Tuesday, Nicholas Cage in *National Treasure* on Wednesday, and Sherlock Holmes on Thursday. I didn't want to sit through a class and a lecture that didn't interest me. I wanted every day to be my own adventure just like a golden retriever, and when my work didn't bring me that adventure, I was disappointed.

As I approached my sophomore year in college, I realized my classes aren't meant to be an adventure, but if I changed my perspective on how I viewed them, I would get closer to the way Gary Vaynerchuk viewed his Monday mornings. I would set out each day to take something meaningful away from each class and store it in my brain for later. In this way, no matter what I was learning, I felt pride in the ability to recall information at a later date from my memory archives.

This seemed to work well for my perspective on my classes, but as I became exposed to the world of internships, job offers, and grad school, I again worried about finding happiness in my work. I discovered I was not alone in this concern.

Allison Gist said as we transition from college into the real world, everyone wants to find a job they enjoy and feel like they fit in. She said, "Work shouldn't be something we dread and can't wait to leave. We should be passionate about our work and use that 64.28 percent for something meaningful, not just to pass the time until the weekend."

What is it like to work in a career field you are passionate about? My best answer at the time was chasing hidden treasure with a metal detector my parents had given me for my eleventh birthday. I had wanted it so badly, and the next day after receiving the gift I was digging up my backyard in search of gold coins.

Friends would come over to my house and we would play for hours in the backyard as we unearthed bits of metal and corroded pennies. We were so excited with every beep of the metal detector and we were ready to dig as far down as we needed to get treasure. It was like I was a golden retriever digging up buried bones in the backyard. This thought made me smile.

My dad and I would also take weekend hikes to different trails near our house and bring a shovel to dig up any findings. I was so sure every time we went out we would discover a long-lost historical item and strike it rich. I just loved the adrenaline, the passion, and the anticipation of digging up a target. I didn't mind the long hours in the sun, getting covered in dirt from the digging, and having people stare at us on the hiking trail. I was so determined to become the next Indiana Jones with that metal detector, and I would've gone out to dig everyday if I could.

Just thinking about those memories makes me smile. That was a long time ago. I still love that metal detector, but it has collected dust in my room over the years as I shifted my focus to my academic, athletic, and social success. Replacing the metal detector and the dream of treasure was projects, finals, and internship applications. I was worried the feeling I had while using the metal detector with my friends in my backyard was gone with the past.

Daniel Caruso related this to his own experience of pursuing his love of film in a career. He said, "If you don't like your job then there's so much pressure on each weekend to make up for that joy you missed out on Monday through Friday. I don't want to feel like any time is wasted, and that's why I'm focusing on pursuing my passion."

I thought about what he said, and as I continued to work it out in my head, I kept coming back to what my friend said about me being a golden retriever. To me, dogs have always been the physical manifestation of happiness. Happiness is hard to describe or define, but no matter how much work I have, when I see a dog being taken for a walk or greeting me as I enter the house, it just makes me happy.

It always seemed like dogs personified the natural happiness Daniel Gilbert explained in his book *Stumbling on Happiness.*[37] Dogs simply want to be loved, and when they receive love, their want is fulfilled and they are naturally happy. Could it really be so simple? It's like every dog has unlocked the secret to consistent happiness, and seeing a dog being taken on a walk or greeting their owner after a day alone was my idea of pure joy as a kid. I wanted to find a balance between that and the hunger and desire to love your work like Gary Vaynerchuk described.

After rescuing my first dog, Lusa, a flat-coat retriever, and later my other dog, Maverick, a golden retriever-husky mix, I looked forward each day to coming home from school to two smiling, furry faces.

My parents, teachers, and friends all experienced happiness and sadness just like I did, but dogs were different. My dogs' happiness was genuine and stemmed from simply getting to live their lives and be loved. I've even had a running joke with my mom that it would be interesting to get to experience being a dog for a day. Were my dogs happy because their lives are so simple? This is a crucial question posed in happiness research.

When I began to immerse myself in my psychological research, this idea of the happiness of dogs rested at the forefront of my mind. For as advanced as human beings are, have dogs solved one of the greatest human mysteries—how to be happy?

My dogs greeted me when I came in the door after school as a kid, when I got home from college, and when I come home at

---

37   Daniel Gilbert, *Stumbling on Happiness* (New York: Vintage Books, 2007).

the end of a workday with the same level of happiness. Their consistent happiness has not wavered throughout the years; it is one of the few constants in my life I can always count on.

No matter how many times my dogs have gone outside in the same backyard, the same block, or the same dog park, they are so unbelievably excited to do so every single time. They are so ridiculously happy to be in the yard or park, and it's like nothing else matters to them in that moment. The place they've walked for years is still new each and every time they visit. I wanted to go to work each day with that same happiness and desire to accomplish my tasks.

As I continued to work through this idea, I had the pleasure of speaking with Keri Goldman, the founder of Paws 4 a Cure. Keri's nonprofit organization provides financial assistance for pet owners across the country who cannot afford veterinary care for their pets. Paws 4 a Cure relies solely on public support and donations and does not receive government funding.

Keri started Paws 4 A Cure as a way to carry on the memory of her Chow, Nikko, who passed away from cancer in 2007. Kerry found when Nikko was diagnosed with cancer, there were no organizations available to offer financial assistance with veterinary care. Because of her love and dedication to Nikko, Keri sold personal belongings and ate from food banks to produce the funds for Nikko's multiple surgeries and follow-up veterinary care.

"Through the tough times in my life, my dog was always there, and Nikko taught me about pure love. Dogs will find a way to bring positivity into your day, and they don't discriminate.

Nikko brought me so much happiness every day in only a way that a dog can," Keri said.

In creating Paws 4 a Cure, Keri wanted to be able to help others facing similar situations with their pets and ensure they had the funds to help. She found her passion in life as she carries on Nikko's memory of happiness and love, ensuring pet owners would not be turned away from necessary veterinarian care for their pet simply because they cannot pay. It's this passion for her work and for helping pet owners that drives Keri to continue working hard on her mission to help pet owners in need.

That passion doesn't simply change because it's a Monday at the start of a workweek, or Friday heading into the weekend. It perseveres because of the love for the work we do. But, of course, we want to have more good days than stressful or boring workdays.

So how can we make the 64.28 percent of our lives from Monday morning to Friday afternoon enjoyable? Let's be honest with ourselves. Even with the job of our dreams, every day will not be enjoyable. We simply want to maximize joy and passion for our work the majority of the time we are working Monday through Friday.

In this maximization of enjoyment Monday through Friday, sometimes the best things happen when we're not expecting them. I know that sounds cliché, but Keri's story is proof our passions can find us and take us down a path we had never imagined. Her love for Nikko and passion for helping others who struggle with paying their vet bills led her down this path for the past thirteen years.

Not every day can be a grand adventure with an exciting arc and plot twist, but Monday through Friday has so much to offer if we make the choice to recognize it. Whatever the passion, let's pursue that path and, in doing so, find how our unique abilities will translate into making an impact in the world. This is how we will create a productive and enjoyable future together: by viewing the 64.28 percent as something to maximize our enjoyment and keeping an open mind to following a path we may not have originally seen.

CHAPTER 9

MY LIFE IS A ROLLER COASTER, BUT UNPREDICTABILITY CREATES OPPORTUNITY

———

"If my life were a song, it would probably be titled 'Roller Coaster,' up and down all the time."

—SCOTTY MCCREERY

It loops, it twists, it turns, it speeds up and slows down, and we aren't sitting in the control booth of the roller coaster of our lives; we are in the front row of the ride. We are strapped into the ride, but we can't see what is coming up next on the tracks. It's no secret life is unpredictable, and we don't know what tomorrow will bring. But just because we are not sitting at the control booth doesn't mean we can't use the unpredictability of our ride to our advantage.

I love roller coasters. I have been drawn to this analogy of likening a roller coaster to life ever since I visited Six Flags Magic Mountain for the first time in third grade with my dad. I was just tall enough to ride almost every roller coaster in the park, and I had my eyes on one in particular, X2. This ride was supposed to be the wildest and most insane ride in the whole park, and my dad and I waited in line for hours to ride it. Every online review we had read prior to coming to the park raved "there is nothing ordinary about X2. It's a different kind of coaster."

Finally, we got to the front of the line as my anticipation and nerves reached its peak. We got on and buckled up. The attendant came by and made sure everything was fastened, and after the "all clear," the coaster started to move. It seemed like as soon as we left the station, we were flying.

The ride was going so fast I legitimately could not see in front of me with the wind whipping me in the face. I was just trying to hold on to dear life as the ride flipped, twisted, and dipped unexpectedly. However, what I remember most was a stoppage in the middle. For a very brief portion, the ride slowed down as if it was building momentum, like a bull pawing the ground before it charges.

My long hair was plastered back from the wind, and I turned to my dad and asked, "Is it over?" with a look of bewilderment on my face. As soon as I finished the question, the ride took off again. Just like the first half of the ride, I was thrown around and couldn't see from the wind hitting my face. Then the ride pulled back into the station and my dad and I moved off the platform. I told my dad the ride was so wild because I couldn't see where we were going and had no way to prepare.

He just laughed and said it was one of the best roller coasters he's ever been on. Neither of us will ever forget that day, but for me it was symbolic. I thought of X2 as a kind of symbol for life. I can't see where I'm going, and it's scary not knowing if I'm on the right path or what will happen next. This idea frequently worried me as I grew up.

Former college baseball player Drew Jansen said, "When you're young, it doesn't take effort to be happy. It's natural. And your worries are so few. But as you get older, you're faced with the realities of people getting sick and dying and all these different social pressures and dramas. That's what causes the anxiety of the uncertainty in life. We've seen what can go wrong and what's bad in the world, and we don't want that to happen to us. It just gives me a bad feeling, so I use positivity to combat this uncertainty, and think one day at a time, this will be a good day."

It was difficult for me to come to terms with the unpredictability of life. What if I got struck by lightning while walking in the rain? What if a shark came up and tried to bite me when I was body surfing? What if I didn't get a tomorrow?

Art Markman, a professor of psychology at the University of Texas at Austin, says in his *Psychology Today* article "Unpredictability Is in Our Nature" that "unpredictability is a fundamental part of human nature." Whether I liked it or not, unpredictability was part of my reality. Markman goes on to explain if unpredictability wasn't part of life, then human beings "would be losing out in the search for the best things that life has to offer."[38]

I recognized I couldn't change life's unpredictability. No one can. But this fact didn't really ease my mind. Author and screenwriter Tinker Lindsey said, "The key is developing the ability to respond to whatever comes up. You have to be flexible in the expectations you have for yourself. The mortality of human beings in life inherently is unpredictable. Our expectations in the face of this unpredictability lead to suffering, but if we let them go and embrace the unpredictability, we can find contentment and acceptance." As I struggled with this, I remembered talking to my dad one day about my concerns with life's unpredictability. I asked him, "How can I feel comfortable with not knowing what will happen next? What if something bad happens next? I want to be ready."

My dad looked at me and said, "What if it was Christmas every day? Or what if it was your birthday every day? What would happen?"

I responded with "I don't know," (but the idea honestly sounded pretty good in my book).

He said, "If it was your birthday every day then it wouldn't be special. If we knew what would happen in life every day, it wouldn't be a life. We would just be existing and following what we are supposed to do. You can blaze your own trail and control how you act. That is the gift life gives to us."

---

38 Art Markman, "Unpredictability Is in Our Nature," *Psychology Today*, November 17, 2008, accessed May 10, 2020.

Wow, I hadn't thought of that way to look at it. With the way my dad described it, now unpredictability created opportunity for each day and each moment rather than fear. He turned unpredictability into a positive thing. I liked that.

This sense of optimism despite unpredictability is echoed by a Workforce Institute at UKG global survey with 3,400 Gen Z participants around the globe. The results showed more than half (56 percent) of Gen Z are "very" or "extremely" optimistic about their professional future.[39]

The optimism of Gen Z's future is even more telling when 32 percent of Gen Z respondents in the global survey say they are the hardest-working generation ever. Additionally, 36 percent of Gen Zers in the survey believe they "had it the hardest" when entering the working world compared to all other generations before it. University of Alabama graduate Charli Sone said, "I have to remind myself to be fun and silly because the real world can suck that away from you. As I grew up, my childhood optimism quickly turned to a realistic view of the world. You don't know what's going to happen. That's our reality. But I'm starting to get that optimism back. In the face of uncertainty, I'm working on being optimistic." In the face of this unpredictability and difficult professional circumstances, the majority of Gen Z remains optimistic about the future.

---

39 "Gen Z Feels They Work the Hardest, Says New Workforce Institute at Kronos Research," *HR Dive*, June 11, 2019, accessed May 8, 2020.

Armed with a new confidence in knowing some of my fellow members of Gen Z viewed life's unpredictability in a positive light, I set out to make the most of each opportunity put in front of me. I quickly found every decision in my life, down to the smallest insignificant ones, will alter my timeline.

Ironically enough, it was around this time I saw the movie *The Matrix* for the first time. Starring Keanu Reeves as Neo and Laurence Fishburne as Morpheus, this movie highlight how our everyday decisions, whether big or small, change our life path.

Neo, who on Earth is called Thomas Anderson, is a successful professional program hacker who is approached by Morpheus. It is Morpheus' job to make sure the destiny of the people around him is fulfilled properly, and he knows Thomas Anderson's destiny is to become Neo and save all of mankind.

At a crucial point in the beginning of the movie, Morpheus offers Neo a choice: take the blue pill or the red pill. The blue pill will allow Neo to return to his normal life as a programmer named Thomas Anderson, but the red pill will give Neo the chance to escape this virtual reality and live in the real world where humans are kept as energy sources for computer intelligence in the Matrix. Whatever choice Neo made in this instance would drastically affect his life path. He chose the red pill and was granted the opportunity into the "real world," and a door he didn't know existed was opened up.

In each decision I made, I began thinking how in an alternate reality, I made a different choice. Was that choice better than the one I made? Should I have made that choice?

After seeing this movie, I began to treat every decision like I was in Neo's position. The simple decision between whether to use almond milk or skim milk in my cereal was now crucial to my success that day. I became focused on making the *correct choice* with every little decision I made throughout my day. In doing so, I felt like I was going insane.

I then thought about the biggest decisions in my life in these terms. I chose my high school, college, and law school over the other options I had. I chose to give up my senior year of college to come home and help my family. I chose to work full-time at a law firm while completing my undergraduate degree. In an alternate reality, would I be happier and would my life be better with different choices?

I wished I had a crystal ball to see how each decision would play out. If I knew how each decision would play out, then I couldn't possibly make a mistake. I would wait for a sign from the universe telling me what to do. The "aha moment" would give me the clarity I desired. I just, above all, didn't want to make any "wrong choices." I didn't want any "what ifs" that would cause regret in my life.

When I made the decision to come home and help my family during my senior year of college, I realized there is no universal "correct choice" in my decisions. Whether or not there is a better choice in a given situation is for me to determine. My indecisiveness was causing me to miss out on potential opportunities because I was spending so much time trying to figure out the *right choice.*

Why were these decisions so hard for me to make? It was because I was trying to control the path of my roller coaster instead of seeing unpredictability as the opportunity my dad presented.

I wanted to do what's best for myself at every single second, but my indecisiveness with everyday choices was causing emotional anguish and mental exhaustion. It turns out this idea is more common than I realized.

It is with this concept of decision-making that Sheena Iyengar, a professor of business at Columbia Business School, analyzes why human beings agonize over certain decisions in her book *The Art of Choosing.* In the book, Iyengar discusses a psychological experiment that she conducted in 2000, which has become one of the most well-known experiments in consumer psychology. In the experiment, a grocery store presents customers with two different sampling stations for jam. One of the sampling stations contains twenty-four different flavors of jam while the other one only contains six options.

Iyengar analyzed the purchasing habits of the customers who passed through and stopped at the tables. The results of the study revealed 30 percent of the consumers who visited the table with six jam options, purchased at least one jar of jam. Contrastingly, of the consumers who visited the sampling station with twenty-four flavors, only 3 percent actually bought a jar of jam. Despite attracting more onlookers,

Iyengar ultimately found "the smaller selection actually generated more sales."[40]

Iyengar maintains the reason behind this phenomenon is human beings' fear of making the wrong choice when they are presented with a wide variety of options. The more choices we have in front of us, the lower the chance we feel we will make the "right" choice compared to a 50/50 decision between two things. Additionally, the "awareness that there may be a better option triggers the urge to find it," according to Iyengar. Using this data, she comes to the conclusion in the study that "human cognitive ability cannot efficiently compare more than five options."

However, there is no "right choice" or "wrong choice" in the majority of the daily choices in our lives. There is only the choice we feel is best to make in that moment. Life will go on, and the world will not cease to spin on its axis because of our decision. It comforted me to know I will always have another decision tomorrow, which will be another opportunity.

With this perspective, now there was no "right option" to agonize over. If there is no right answer, then we don't have to worry about making the "wrong" choice. We can visualize the result of each choice all we want, but whatever option we don't choose, we will have no idea what our lives would have been like if we made that choice. Alternate reality is not available for our viewing.

---

40 "Reduce the Options You Give Your Customers and Get 30% More Conversions," *Usability Testing* (blog), Conversion Hub, accessed May 16, 2020.

This perspective helps us alleviate the fear of making a choice we will regret because we are choosing what will be best for us in that moment. Similarly, this way of thinking helps us trust ourselves more in our decision-making capabilities. With each decision, we first need to get to the core of the issue and dissect it so we can trust ourselves and feel comfortable to make our choice.

For Gen Z, like all other generations, we do not know what lies ahead on our roller coaster. When each of our roller coasters ride smoothly in a straight line on the tracks, the decisions are easier. But whatever unpredictability the roller coaster presents us with, we will hold on tight to the handlebars and take advantage of the opportunities we've been given. We want to change the world, but not every choice is a life-or-death, Earth shattering decision we need to make. One day at a time, we can take advantage of the opportunities our roller coasters have given us, and we can smile knowing although we can't see the tracks ahead, we possess the skills to seize our future.

CHAPTER 10

BEFORE IT WAS SURVIVING, BUT TODAY IT'S THRIVING

———

"The meaning of life is not simply to exist, to survive, but to move ahead, to go up, to achieve, to conquer."
—ARNOLD SCHWARZENEGGER

Don't just survive, thrive. Such a simple phrase, but where is the line we cross over from living, breathing, and existing to thriving? That line often gets blurred, erased, and redrawn as society's expectations for Gen Z continue to increase. If that's the case, what is *thriving* and how does it come about in our lives?

Growing up, my parents taught me to work hard and aim high in everything I set my mind to. They said by working hard and chasing my dreams, there was nothing I could not accomplish. In chasing my dreams, they told me I should always strive to exceed expectations because anything worth doing, is worth doing with 100 percent effort.

It was first in high school I began to recognize I wasn't alone in my ambitious pursuit of life goals. I was surrounded by a class of students who shared my same mindset. I was surrounded by kids who appeared to be working hard every day to realize their athletic, academic, and professional dreams. It was difficult to stand out from the crowd.

I met students who had started and operated their own successful businesses, set off on multiple community service immersions to other countries during holiday breaks, and I even knew a few students who received awards from the president for their achievements.

Author of *Generation Optimism* Juan David Campolargo, who has been an inspiration to me in writing this book, started his own small hedge fund, wrote his first novel, and spoke at his first two TEDx Talks among other achievements, all before graduating high school!

Juan and the other students I met each found their own unique way to thrive. It was not enough to have a strong work ethic, be athletic, and be smart. I found it harder to thrive in my unique way as rejection became more frequent.

I specifically remember this happening at a college baseball showcase I attended my junior year of high school. One of the top colleges on my list was there, and I was determined to impress the coach. I had one of the best showcases of my life, and I confidently went up to talk to the coach of my top school afterward.

I explained to him it was my dream to play there, and I wanted to know if he thought I would be a fit for their program. He looked at me and said, "I liked what I saw, but you're not big enough. We're only taking guys over six feet tall that hit for power. I'm sorry. Good luck."

That was a gut busting shot to the solar plexus. I wasn't what they were looking for, which I had no control over.

Many of my friends who were student athletes in high school and college experienced the same struggle of rejection and temporary defeat. Former collegiate soccer player Kelsy Haden said, "Rejection by coaches would always hurt because you did everything you could on the field and put yourself out there. You get your hopes up, and when it doesn't work out, it's really hard. you feel like there was something you did wrong, and after being rejected it's easy to get down on yourself and believe you're not good enough. That's why you can't stop; you have to keep going."

This was coming at a time when college was quickly approaching, and I felt immense pressure to perform academically and athletically to have the future success I desired. My high school counselor told me top colleges were looking for unique students to increase their student diversity and "specialness of the student population." He explained colleges see thousands of students with fantastic grades, volunteer work, and extracurriculars.

Similarly, my high school and club baseball coaches told me collegiate programs were not only looking for great players. They were looking for well-rounded players in all facets of their game.

For both academics and athletics, the same question arose: How could I *thrive*?

The *Fight or Flight Theory* developed by Harvard psychiatrist Walter Cannon was the basis for the idea human beings had developed a unique survival mechanism connected to their self-awareness. If we perceive a situation as dangerous or stressful, we make the conscious choice to stay and fight or run away based on what will be most beneficial in that moment.

That is pretty amazing. For each challenge human beings have faced through millions of years of evolution, our brains have become hardwired to help us *survive*. Surviving has transitioned from a goal to an instinct as human beings began to advance and further adapt to the world.

Industrial and technological advancement improved the quality of life. Access to technology and health care has decreased the annual mortality rate, from one in forty-two people in 1900 to one in one hundred twenty-five people by 1998, a cumulative decline of 67 percent.[41]

---

41   David R. Francis, "Why Do Death Rates Decline?" The National Bureau of Economic Research, accessed Apr. 24, 2020.

With our population increasing to nearly eight billion individuals worldwide in the near future, our life focus has shifted from our ancestors' focus. Today we have a desire for *optimization* of our lives. In moving from simply wanting to live to wanting to live the best life possible, human beings are shifting from *surviving to thriving.*

According to sociologist and author of *Startup Your Life: Hustle and Hack Your Way to Happiness,* Anna Akbari explains the difference between surviving and thriving is quite simple. Akbari says, "Surviving is a grim struggle—you're white-knuckling life, just barely getting by. Thriving is living and thinking abundantly. Surviving is a drag, a daily slog to stay alive. Thriving is joyful and infectious."[42]

My desire to thrive like those around me created a reality where I based my ability to thrive on other peoples' opinions. If I received negative feedback from a parent, teacher, or coach, it must mean I wasn't thriving and I needed to improve.

Each "no" and academic, athletic, or social rejection, I took to heart. Every time I got turned down, it felt personal. It felt like my work and my desire just didn't cut it. On its face, each rejection felt like they were saying to my face "you're not good enough."

But I wasn't alone. Texas Christian University graduate Michael Vogeler says, "There's always going to be people that

---

42   Anna Akbari, "Surviving vs. Thriving," *Psychology Today,* Sussex Publishers, December 16, 2019, accessed May 14, 2020.

tell you 'no' and don't think you can achieve what you want to. During the bad times, you just can't believe those people because they're wrong. Find your driving force. My driving force every day when I wake up is to put myself in the best position to make my dreams come true in any way I can. I want that success because I know if I can be successful, then that will spread to those around me as well."

For Gen Z, there is a strong generational connection to this idea. *UNiDAYS*, an England-based marketing company, conducted a survey with 16,747 college-aged members of Gen Z from the US, UK, Australia, and New Zealand. The findings showed "93 percent of Gen Zers believe they're either 'empowered' or 'somewhat empowered' to shape 'what [their] future will be'." Additionally, "roughly 53 percent of Gen Zers agree that 'personal success' is the most important thing in life."[43]

The idea of thriving I had previously coveted now felt increasingly more difficult to attain, and this process of thriving would only get more difficult as I transitioned from college to the real world. I felt constantly on display and judged for my actions. After a baseball showcase I would wonder, "did I show them what they're looking for?" and in college when I applied to internships I asked myself, "did I show them why I'm different?"

I was told I needed to stand out and differentiate myself, which is exactly what I tried to do. I tried to thrive rather than just survive, but with each rejection academically and

---

43   "Gen Z: Preparing to Face the Future," UniDAYS, accessed Mar. 29, 2020.

athletically, I got down on myself. I was losing faith in my abilities.

But I was very surprised to find out I wasn't alone in my fixation on thriving. Current University of Colorado Boulder senior Sophia Gardinier said, "I know I'm 'thriving' when I am both mentally and physically excelling. It's holistic, and I feel at peace. I want to thrive in my career, and I want to know that I am making a difference in people's lives."

It helped to know I wasn't alone and other people thought this was hard, too. They wanted to thrive just like I did but were being brought down by the setbacks and rejections. Yet despite this struggle, 88 percent of Gen Z still says, "their generation has the power to change the world for the better," according to the 2019 Porter Novelli/Cone Gen Z Purpose Study. Amidst all the rejection and the repeated "no's" it amazed me the overwhelming majority of Gen Z still believes we can thrive together.[44]

The sense of generational optimism amidst the negativity of rejection brought me hope. Other members of my generation shared my same desire to make an impact on the world we are inheriting. Despite facing the stresses and pressures of life as well as a tumultuous job market, this sense of optimism shared by my generational peers spurred me to put less emphasis on other's judgments of me.

---

44 "90 Percent of Gen Z Tired of How Negative and Divided Our Country Is Around Important Issues, According to Research by Porter Novelli/ Cone," *Yahoo! Finance*, Yahoo, October 23, 2019, accessed Apr. 15, 2020.

University of California, Berkeley graduate Matt Bland said, "You apply to hundreds and hundreds of jobs, and you may get rejection letters from all of them. Or maybe they'll engage in the interview process, and they'll turn you down during the final round of interviews, which is like really heartbreaking. But then you realize that you made it this far. And that's farther than everyone else came. Yeah, you didn't make it past that last step, but it's encouraging. I think I use synthetic happiness in those situations a lot because it's a negative that I didn't get the job, but it makes me happy knowing that I got so close. And one day, I have the faith I will get that job that's right for me."

Talking to my friends gave me strength, and learning my generation still believes we can better the world around us motivated me. I no longer wanted to give others the power to affect my happiness. It was tearing me up, and I wasn't able to please everyone. What one person said they thought I did a great job in, there's always someone else who says the opposite. By basing my feeling of personal success on others' views of me, this mindset made it so I didn't have a chance to thrive. Because I wanted to thrive so badly, every setback and detour from the path I envisioned muddied the waters of my process to achieve my goals.

I realized these judgments were based off other people's viewpoints of me. When I was rejected from a school or an internship offer, the admissions office or employer didn't even know me. They were simply making a decision based on an application and what they thought would be best for their school or company.

Instead of predicating our mood on how an admissions office or potential employer views us, we can understand our self-worth and the external pressures we feel are of our own creation. By shifting our focus inward on our comfortability in our own skin and our own personal judgments, then we can set our path to thriving.

By becoming personally accountable for creating a path toward our goals, we can lean into the optimism shared by our fellow members of Gen Z to encourage positive change in the world. We are now making decisions for ourselves and no one else. We recognize what our strengths and weaknesses are as a generation, and we no longer need others' validation or praise to feel we're thriving.

As the old adage goes, we are "the captain of our ship," and we can make the conscious choice to use each rejection as motivation. Yeah, it's hard to keep your chin up when you repeatedly get sand kicked in your face, but as a member of Gen Z, we will face many obstacles and rejections as we continue to grow. Each "no" we have received was like a Northern star leading us to where we are today.

Our sense of optimism as we enter the real world is the driving force allowing us to thrive in the world we are inheriting. Rejection doesn't mean we failed; failure was necessary for our growth. Focusing on thriving doesn't mean we have to be the best at every single thing we do. We just have to be the best version of ourselves each day to thrive in the way we want.

CHAPTER 11

NEGATIVITY IS POWERFUL, BUT I FEED MY GOOD WOLF MORE

"Going through things you never thought you'd go through, will only take you places you never thought you'd get to"
—MORGAN HARPER NICHOLS

Sometimes darkness can seem all-encompassing, and a feeling of hopelessness lingers around as if to suggest things will never get better; this negativity is now our life. Saying "every storm runs out of rain" and "there's a light at the end of the tunnel" seems like wishful thinking when we're in the eye of the storm and the pitch-black tunnel. So do we just miserably wait for enough time to pass for our wounds to heal into scars? No, we *flip the script.*

My Uncle Michael was diagnosed with stage four cancer on the same weekend I played the opening game of my junior year college baseball season. We had traveled to North

Carolina for the weekend series, and I got a phone call from my mom the night we returned to campus explaining the news. This had come on top of hearing my maternal grandfather was getting worse, and my mom and maternal grandmother were struggling.

I didn't know this would be my last spring spent at college with my friends and teammates. I couldn't imagine that weekend would be my last opening day and that spring my last baseball season. It wasn't supposed to be like that. My family wasn't supposed to hurt so badly, and I wasn't supposed to watch the people I care about slowly die. This wasn't what I had imagined life's script looking like. It felt like a cruel director's cut.

I came home from school the summer between my junior and senior year of college and made the decision not to return in the fall to help take care of my family. This decision made me feel like I retook the control life had stripped from my family, but it didn't change the fact I knew I would soon lose people I cared about.

My maternal grandfather and Uncle Michael were both in the delivery room when I was born. They cared about me and loved me. They were my family. Now their days consisted of pain and suffering from their diseases. I couldn't imagine I would be spending the weeknights of my senior year of college taking care of family members on hospice rather than with friends, but I did. I couldn't picture my grandfather not recognizing me, or losing all of his memories of me growing up, but that's what happened. He didn't remember anything.

"This is like a bad dream that I just want to wake up from," my mom would say when there was an especially bad day. This was true. It didn't feel real. The absolute worst part of it all was I knew what was coming. I knew my time with my grandfather and my uncle was dwindling. While I saw videos of my friends and teammates enjoying college on social media, I was helping my grandfather walk to the bathroom and grabbing a plastic bag for my Uncle Michael to throw up in (a side effect of his chemotherapy).

There was so much negativity infused into their situations—with the added stress of medical bills and coordinating caregiver schedules—it felt like the light of positivity was extinguished. It was hard to see any good in losing two people I loved while at the same time missing my senior year of college and my last year of collegiate athletics.

My focus became enjoying every moment I had left with them, which is exactly what I tried to do. Most nights I lay awake, trying to figure out my situation like it was a riddle. If I could solve it, maybe things would get better. Irrational, I know, but I didn't know what else to do. I kept looking for a sign everything would all be okay.

Instead, I witnessed two moments. In these moments, one from my grandfather and one from my Uncle Michael, I saw a sliver of positivity truly can create a silver lining which makes the darkness easier to deal with. In the storm of my life, these moments were a ray of sunshine.

A few days before he passed, my grandfather laid in his hospice bed staring intently up at the ceiling. He had been staring at the same spot for a long time until my mom asked him what he was staring at. He said, "the beach" and pointed up at the spot he was staring at on the ceiling. He said, "There's boats on the water, and it's beautiful." He hadn't talked in days, but as he described what he saw to my mom, I could feel his wonderment. It sounded serene and peaceful. He was near death, but in that moment, I knew he wasn't in pain anymore. That was my silver lining.

I couldn't change him getting Alzheimer's disease, and I couldn't prevent his death, but I could change how I chose to view it. That gave me comfort, and when he died two days later, the silver lining became emblazoned in my memory.

For my Uncle Michael, I took this silver lining and tried to be a light of positivity for him, but it was so hard. It's painful to watch someone you care about suffer and you don't know how to help. But I still tried.

On one of the days I visited him during hospice, I read my first rough draft chapter of this book to him, and as usual he pointed out all the edits he recommended (he used to be an editor). As my mom and I walked out, she saw something on his desk near the door we hadn't noticed before. It was a silver figurine about four inches tall.

The figurine had a platform base and an archway extending upward on both sides, connected at the top by a beam. In the middle of the archway was a door. It was bolted onto the archway on the left side but was free on all other sides so you could move it in an out of the archway like a real door. When opened fully, the door gave way to an open archway, and when closed, the door appeared strong and solid.

Just above the protruding doorknob, two words were scrawled across the face of the door: Another Opens.

I thought about the meaning behind this and knew it had to be connected to the phrase "When one door closes, another door opens." How poetic and timely at this point in my life. My college door and my baseball door were closed. My Uncle Michael's door of life was about to close, and I couldn't stick my foot out and stop it from shutting.

There were a lot of doors appearing to close, and I didn't see any opening. But as I sat next to Uncle Michael's bed one night, I tried to envision another door opening. I talked to him even though he was asleep, and I like to think he could hear me. I said my goodbyes and received a call from my mom he had passed away hours after I had left.

I hung up and tried to process the words. His door had closed like my grandpa's did just months before. As I thought about how I couldn't ever give them another hug, another thought came to the forefront of my mind. It came from Uncle Michael's silver figurine. Maybe up there, their doors are forever open, and they are free of the pain and suffering they felt in this world. This was the silver lining, and it gave me comfort.

The negativity I felt was eating me alive before I found the silver linings. Where I thought the doors around me were closing one by one, it was because I was looking through the binoculars. The silver linings allowed me to put my glasses back on and see there is always an open door. This concept of silver linings became almost like an obsession, and I wanted to learn how to spot them in every situation in my life.

I turned to former professional baseball player and owner of Baseball Central, TJ Runnells who said, "You don't know what's going to happen at any moment, so you need to live every day for that day. It's one thing to say you're optimistic and a positive person, but it's another to act like it. If you act it, the energy will flow around you, and others will see it. Be disciplined in your creation of positivity and be accountable to your own happiness in life."

My search took me to Matthew McConaughey's commencement speech at the University of Houston in 2014. In his speech, McConaughey shares with his audience his interpretation of a famous story from a Cherokee tribe which says we all have two wolves inside of us, a good one and a bad one. The good wolf represents our positivity and light while the bad wolf represents negativity and darkness. McConaughey says in his interpretation "they *both* wanna eat" and "we just gotta feed that good wolf a little more than the other one."

Negative events are inevitable. For Gen Z, we are no strangers to the dark wolf being fed more than the good ones by negative events in our lives. When I asked him about this internal dichotomy between the good wolf and bad wolf, current California Polytechnic State student Bo Henderson said, "No one wants it to, but the bad wolf will come into our lives at certain points and we often don't control that. What we do control is having the strength to see past it and not give in. The good wolf has the power to win out; it just sometimes needs a little help."

As we grew up in a post 9/11 world and attended school, Gen Z witnessed forty-two school shootings, totaling a death toll of 330 victims, according to data platform Statista. Psychological research shows these negative events early on in the lives of Gen Z were significant in shaping our views of the world.[45]

In fact, "75 percent of Gen Z members said that mass shootings are a significant source of stress," according to a survey conducted online by The Harris Poll on behalf of the American Psychological Association in July and August 2018 an additional 21 percent of Gen Z respondents said the prospect of a shooting occurring at their school was a "constant or frequent source of stress."[46]

The majority of Gen Z is too young to remember the Columbine High School shooting in 1999 which left twelve students and one teacher dead, but multiple school shootings have scarred our memory as we grew up.

I was in fourth grade when the school shooting at Virginia Tech University occurred in Blacksburg, Virginia in 2007. This event left thirty-two students dead. I was in my first

45 Katharina Buchholz, "Infographic: Number of School Shootings Increased Every Decade," *Statista Infographics*, November 15, 2019, accessed May 12, 2020.
46 "APA Stress in America Survey: Generation Z Stressed About Issues in the News but Least Likely to Vote," American Psychological Association, October 30, 2018, accessed Mar. 30, 2020.

semester of high school when the Sandy Hook elementary school shooting in Newton, Connecticut left twenty young children and six staff members dead. Just two years ago, I watched on the news as a reporter confirmed a school shooting at Stoneman Douglas High School in Parkland, Florida had left seventeen dead.

These moments are real, and Gen Z has borne witness to the heartbreak and sadness following these school shootings. In these moments, the bad wolf is fed and grows stronger than the good wolf. The bad wolf can be relentless in its pursuit of control over our lives and our relationships, and it has many friends. The bad wolf gives us stress, heartbreak, regret, sadness, and death to change our thinking for the worse.

The ancient Greek poet Aeschylus says, "There is no pain so great as the memory of joy in present grief." We are sad when someone dies because we realize all those happy memories don't "happen anymore." You won't be able to make new memories. Those memories which in the moment were pure bliss are now a painful reminder of the permanence of death.

Similarly, when a relationship ends, it hurts to think what that person could have been like in our future. Saying "everything happens for a reason" or "things will get better" just doesn't cut it in these moments. It is easy to think time doesn't heal all wounds and getting over the negativity is impossible. In such a moment, anger and heartbreak feel eternal and all-encompassing.

But we are all human beings, and we all feel. When someone we care about passes away, it is sad. When a relationship we valued ends, the natural human response is to feel the wave of sadness. TJ told me, "Sit and talk with yourself. Be honest about how you're feeling. You're in the driver's seat in life, but you never know when there will be a roadblock. When you hit that roadblock remember that you're the one that dictates the optimism in your life. It's not easy, but if you understand yourself and you know what you're trying to do, it becomes a way of life."

TJ reminded me why the story from the Cherokee tribe explains there's a reason why two wolves are inside of us. The bad wolf represents every emotion imaginable we do not like to feel, but it is necessary to have in our lives. If everyone lived forever, life wouldn't have the same value and meaning. If nothing bad ever happened, there could be no good because goodness would just be the norm. Our bad days and our failures make our good days and our successes worth it.

I remember getting so sad when I was a little kid because our family vacation would end. On the plane ride home, all I could think about was going back to school soon and it would be a long time before another family vacation. Every time my dad would say, "If you were on a vacation every day, then it wouldn't be special anymore," he was right.

Each negative moment and failure in our lives are Northern Stars guiding us forward on our life path, should we choose to persevere and shift the energy back to the good wolf. As motivational speaker Rich Keller says, "Our negative moments are moments of growth. They always make the good times better."

Recognizing silver linings are a way to feed the good wolf even when it seems like the bad wolf is the stronger one. Silver linings are the cracks of light breaking through the darkness of negativity. After a moment of negativity, we are most vulnerable and susceptible to the energy of the bad wolf. This is the most important time to feed the good wolf because it will be needing it. It is a choice each of us will always have.

In speaking with award-winning leadership blogger Joseph Lalonde, he told me silver linings aren't just associated with a positive outlook; they are an integral form of human communication for expressing our emotions. He said, "When we see a situation through the lens of a silver lining, even in the darkest of times, that little sliver of light will become more apparent, and over time that will grow into something amazing."

Each wolf is there to remind us the importance of embracing our emotions when we feel them. It is great when the good wolf is being fed and we feel good inside, but the balance will eventually shift back to the bad wolf when it is fed next. It is when the bad wolf takes over we can truly see how far our positivity stretches and how much our silver linings matter.

My grandfather and Uncle Michael were two people to whom I dedicated this book in the beginning. I was incredibly fortunate to have had these amazing people in my life for so long. This book is also for every person who has had a positive impact on my life and helped feed my good wolf. These people have been the rays of positivity shining through the darkness of negativity in life when I couldn't see it. They helped me see the silver lining in my life. Feed the good wolf, be the ray of light shining on through, and know no matter how many doors close around you, *another opens* sometimes when you least expect it.

CHAPTER 12

MONEY IS IMPORTANT, BUT FOR GEN Z, CASH IS KING

——

"Money is neither my God or my Devil. It is a form of energy that tends to make us more of who we already are, whether it's greedy or loving."

—DAN MILLMAN

As I write this chapter, I am sitting in my chair on Wednesday May 19, 2020. The TV is on across the room, and the headline at the bottom of the screen underneath the anchorman reads, "Over 1.5 million US Cases and over 5 million world cases of the COVID-19 Virus." We are in the midst of a global pandemic which has claimed the lives of hundreds of thousands of people worldwide.

The virus has also caused the stock market crash of 2020. The virus began on Monday, March 9, with history's largest point plunge for the Dow Jones Industrial Average (DJIA) up to date according to the S&P Dow Jones Indices. In the following days, the US saw two more record-setting point drops on March 12 and March 16, resulting in the three worst point drops in US history.[47]

On March 11, the World Health Organization officially labeled COVID-19 an international pandemic. On the same day, the Dow closed down 20.3 percent from its previous February 12 high. This launched a bear market of falling prices and ended the eleven-year bull market which encouraged buying beginning in March 2009.[48]

I'll be honest. Right now, it's not looking good for Generation Z and our immediate financial future looks bleak. The rising unemployment rate and mass job loss are both "devastation unseen since the Great Depression" according to the *New York Times*. As we enter the job market, these are the major challenges we face in attempting to become financially independent members of society.

If we can't even leave our houses and so many employers are putting hiring freezes on their businesses, what can we do? We don't want to live with our parents forever. How can we make money in a job market like this?

Golfer at University of California, Santa Barbara Brandon Bueno said, "Financial security is the ultimate goal. With financial security I can take care of myself and my family comfortably. Financial security means freedom, but without

---

47 Kimberly Amadeo, "How Does the 2020 Stock Market Compare With Others?" *The Balance*, Apr. 27, 2020, accessed May 19, 2020.
48 Ibid.

that money, that's where the stress comes in. And with COVID-19 right now, that stress is hitting us hard."

Money is a savior and a destroyer—both a blessing and a curse. It is needed for survival, and once secure, money can bring us leisure. Enough of it can make our wildest material dreams come true, and a lack of money can bring us to our knees begging for more. Boston College graduate Henry Hawley added, "Colleges promise you a return on investment from your education. You want to be able to do enjoyable work and love your job, but at the end of the day, you need money to live. Now with COVID-19, our trajectory for long-term financial outlook for our future has completely shifted." It's truly amazing how powerful pieces of colored paper and little metal coins can be.

The Great Recession in 2008 occurred near the middle of my life when I was ten years old. I didn't understand what was happening at the time, but I could tell something was wrong. I remember seeing the words "Great Recession" and "Housing Bubble Burst" on the news. I remember hearing my parents talk about "finances" and "bills" at home as they went over these pieces of paper on the kitchen counter. I also noticed how other parents, when I carpooled with friends or went over to their house, seemed to be bothered by something. I didn't get it.

Looking back, I now understand why they were concerned. The 2008 Recession brought a wave of economic uncertainty. I think this is said best by former General Electric CEO and millionaire Jack Welch. When asked about his rules for life success, he responded, "number one, cash is king."

In late 2018, in their Annual Stress in America Report, the American Psychological Association found of every generation in the study, Gen Z reported the worst overall mental health. A staggering 91 percent of the Gen Zers in the survey reported "they had felt physical or emotional symptoms, such as depression or anxiety, associated with stress."[49]

Brandon Bueno further commented on this by saying, "Our financial opportunities have significantly decreased now, and everyone's kind of scrambling to find that balance of financial security. It's tough right now to see what that looks like."

Although many of us in Gen Z were too young to understand what happened in the 2008 Recession, as we grew up, we have seen money is important and needs to be secured. Our hard work in academics was supposed to lead to the start of a meaningful career. Gen Z wants to become financially independent from our parents and start our new chapter in the real world, but that costs money.

In transitioning from college to the real world, the priority of the utmost importance is finding a secure job with a consistent salary. As the American Psychological Association data shows, money and financial security are critical for Gen Z. But in this current job market, obtaining cash, let alone finding a stable job, has become increasingly difficult.

This situation is unfair and frustrating, but we don't have a choice. This is our reality now. This is the world we inherit,

---

49 "APA Stress in America™ Survey: Generation Z Stressed About Issues in the News but Least Likely to Vote," American Psychological Association, October 30, 2018, accessed Mar. 31, 2020.

and it will be a long road to get back to where we want things to be. But in the face of every obstacle COVID-19 has thrown at the world, Gen Z has a choice in this moment.

The generations preceding us are no stranger to economic obstacles. Lisa B. Kahn, an economics professor at the University of Rochester, conducted a study in 1970 and 1980 where she tracked young white men who graduated from college during a recession. Over the next two decades, Kahn found these men got stuck in low-quality, low-paying jobs if they were able to get a job at all. Additionally, even after the economy recovered, they had a hard time moving into better jobs."[50]

Till von Wachter of the University of California, Los Angeles, and Hannes Schwandt of Northwestern University built on Kahn's study, following Americans who entered the labor market in 1981 and 1982, during the largest postwar recession up to that time.

They discovered those entering the job market not only earned less in midlife, but "they were also less likely to be married or to have children, and more likely to die young, recording higher mortality rates starting in their 30s." Anne Case and Angus Deaton, two scholars from Princeton University, have deemed this phenomenon the "deaths of despair."[51]

50   Eduardo Porter and David Yaffe-Bellany, "Facing Adulthood With an Economic Disaster's Lasting Scars," *The New York Times*, The New York Times, May 19, 2020, accessed May 20, 2020.

51   Ibid.

Their studies show the negative results of a job market after a recession for recent college graduates, but there are those who have found a way to persevere and thrive after an economic collapse. The Silent Generation was born into the Great Depression, the worst economic disaster in US history. Lasting nearly a full decade from 1929 to 1939. The members of the Silent Generation fought through the Dust Bowl and World War II, and their dedication to creating a fruitful future paid off. The Silent Generation went on to promote the idea of the "American Dream" and make the 1950s one of the most prosperous decades in US history, following the completion of World War II. They turned a depression into a recovery as they persevered through the economic challenges put in front of them.

So it is possible. This situation is unfair and frustrating, but we don't have a choice. This is our reality now. This is the world we inherit, and it will be a long road to get back to where we want things to be. But in the face of every obstacle COVID-19 has thrown at the world, Gen Z has a choice in this moment.

The COVID-19 pandemic is affecting the lives of millions around the world, not just us. However, this doesn't mean our futures are a lost cause and we can chalk up our foreseeable obstacles to bad luck. We can and will say, even while faced with all these challenges, "We can succeed, and we will find a way to be happy." That's not wishful thinking, it's accepting the reality of our situation and maintaining the desire to will our professional pursuits into reality despite what's going on in the world.

When my aspirations of playing professional sports didn't materialize, I wanted to find a job I was passionate about which would also give me financial security. I sought to marry the idea of garnering enough money to be financially successful and stable while also being happy in life. I felt like my path may lead to financial success or to happiness, but I had a hard time seeing how it could lead to both.

I wanted to be happy in life, but I also couldn't escape the fact I desired money to become financially secure. University of Alabama graduate Finn Veje said, "It can sometimes feel like a sacrificial tradeoff between being happy and making the most money you can. Living a happy life is liberating and doesn't cost a dime, but meaningfulness in life does cost money. You need money for a family, a house, and comfortability, so it's hard sometimes to think about the intersection between money and happiness." I searched for an answer to ease my mind about how I could have both the financial security and the happiness I desired.

In 2015, Matthew McConaughey gave a commencement speech at the University of Houston. He recounts visiting Southern Louisiana and coming across a voodoo shop. Inside the voodoo shop, McConaughey noticed a wooden partition along one of the walls. Separated into sections was a series of magic potions in vials.

McConaughey says, "The headings above the potions defined what they would give you were things like fertility, health, family, legal help, energy, forgiveness, money." McConaughey smiles and asks the audience, "Guess which column is empty?" After he paused he says, "Money! Let's admit it. Money is king today. It makes the world go round. It is success. The more we have, the more successful we are."

McConaughey goes on to say, "I would argue that our cultural values have even been financialized. It's a get rich quick on the Internet, rich is fifteen minutes of fame world that we live in, and we see it every day." He was right. Cash is king, and most people want to find ways to maximize the money they make in life.

I found it so interesting of all the options McConaughey named, *money* was the empty section of the partition. The money section was empty while the magic potions in the *fertility* and *forgiveness* sections still had vials ready to be taken. Is *money* so important people will choose it over *health* and *family*. It reinforced how powerful and desirable money is and fueled my fire to find a way to get it.[52]

So I thought about ways to get financial security. Winning the lottery would probably solve my financial problems right? It's the needle in a haystack, but with those millions I would be set. Then happiness wouldn't be an issue.

However, it has become fairly well publicized many lottery winners actually aren't happy after they win. A recent study in late 2018 by researchers from the Stockholm School of Economics at Stockholm University and New York University looked at the levels of happiness and satisfaction in winners of the lottery. The researchers initially "hypothesized that

---

52 Matthew McConaughey, "Matthew McConaughey to Grads: Always Play Like an Underdog," *Time*, Time, May 17, 2015, accessed May 20, 2020.

lottery money would make the large prize winners happier and improve their mental health." They asked more than 3,300 participants who had collectively won $277 million in different lotteries a series of questions. The participants had won their lump sums in the past five to twenty-two years, respectively.

The researchers asked the participants, "All things considered, how happy would you say you are?" Then they asked, "Taking all things together in your life, how satisfied would you say that you are with your life these days?" Lastly, they asked participants how often they had experienced a negative or positive emotion in the last two weeks.

The participants' answers to these questions revealed their massive increases in wealth "had a greater impact on over-all life satisfaction and financial satisfaction than it did on happiness and mental health." Robert Ostling, an associate professor at the Institute for International Economic Studies at Stockholm University, explained "life satisfaction" refers to how people feel about the quality of their lives overall, whereas "happiness" measured respondents' day-to-day feelings." Ostling concluded the results of the study "suggest it is more difficult to affect happiness than life satisfaction."[53]

I was surprised by these results, and this disconnect between money and happiness didn't seem to make sense. I've seen how sad and despairing adults are when they lose money,

---

53   Gina Martinez "Everything You Know About the Fate of Lottery Winners Is Probably Wrong," *Time*, Time, October 18, 2018, accessed May 23, 2020.

so why doesn't the financial security of winning the lottery make them happy?

It reminded me of my parents telling me as I grew up, "money won't buy you happiness." This statement gave me a wholly negative connotation toward money, but I knew I would still need it in life. Yes, I need money to survive, and if I make enough I can buy myself the things I want. But the question was how we could fit happiness into the equation. What can we do to be happy during these uncertain economic times?

The answer I came up with was *passion*. If I am passionate about my work, not only would I do it better, but the money I earn would mean more than just financial security. With passion, I would inherently be happy doing work each day. There are many professional careers which can bring financial security and can additionally pay for the luxuries in life. However, a career stemming from passion is different.

For so long, I thought it was a choice between money and happiness. Since I knew I needed money, happiness took a back seat.

But with the uncertainty of the job market due to COVID-19 and the safer-at-home regulations, we don't have a choice. This is a harsh reality, but we need to be realistic. We are inheriting a world in the midst of a pandemic, and we want to find success and monetary gain during one of the worst economic periods in US history. So what can we do right now? Find what we're passionate about because it's what we will want to work toward. I am passionate about the topics in this book and sharing my voice with others, and when I think about the current troubles Gen Z faces today, I know the happiness in doing the work, not the money, will make the difference.

CHAPTER 13

TECHNOLOGY ALLOWS US TO FACETIME, BUT GEN Z WANTS FACE TIME

"Never before in history has innovation offered promise of so much to so many in so short a time."

—DAN MILLMAN

We as Gen Zers are the technology generation, the social media generation, the iPhone generation, and the video game generation. What was life before cell phones, Play Stations, and a bevy of apps at the tip of our fingers? Well, the answer is Gen Z really doesn't know because we were born into the "technology age" and American global network infrastructure provider CommScope Inc. even reports Gen Z is "the most technology-intimate and connectivity-dependent demographic in history."[54]

---

54 "Reader Opinion: CommScope Research on Gen Z Reveals an Always-On Mindset," *Inside Towers*, October 18, 2017, accessed May 19, 2020.

Generation Z is widely considered a cohort of tech-savvy individuals who are the beneficiaries of decades of technological advancement. In a study by Dell Technologies, researchers found 80 percent of people eighteen to twenty-three years old said they aspire to work with cutting-edge technology in their professional careers. An overwhelming 91 percent of Gen Zers in the study responded, "technology will influence their job choice among similar employment offers."[55]

According to *Pew Research*, only 14 percent of US adults had access to the internet in 1995. This number significantly increased to over 87 percent by 2014. Pew Research additionally says, "Generation Z is growing up during the most accelerated and game-changing periods of technological advancements in human history." As many members of Gen Z are beginning to make the transition from college to the real world, companies around the world compete every day to churn out the latest and greatest new piece of technology for public consumption.[56]

However, I didn't truly see how much technology has impacted our lives until one night when I went out to dinner with friends during the summer between my freshman and sophomore year of college. It was a normal Saturday night, and we had gotten reservations at a fun Mexican restaurant in Los Angeles. We met at my friend's house and called an

55   Stars Insider, "How Much Do You Know about Generation Z?" *MSN*, Microsoft News, accessed May 21, 2020.

56   Konrad Krawczyk,"87 Percent of U.S. Adults Use the 'net, and Other Fun Pew Research Stats," *Digital Trends*, February 27, 2014, accessed May 21, 2020.

Uber XL to take us to dinner. It was during this Uber ride I noticed something very interesting.

We had carried our conversation from outside into the car, but within five minutes the car was silent. I was in the back row, so I had a view of everyone in the car. It was silent because every single one of my friends in the car was staring down at their phones. This period of silence lasted for a brief moment and the conversation picked up again when the phones went back in the pocket.

We got to the restaurant and placed our drink and food order after being seated. We struck up a new conversation and talked across the table for fifteen minutes. As the conversation died down, I noticed the same thing I had on the Uber ride over to the restaurant. The table was silent because my friends had pulled out their phones to text someone back or check social media.

I knew I had been guilty of this many times, but I stopped and thought about what this meant. My friends weren't intending to be rude, but they were prioritizing their phones over our time together. Their attachment to their phones seemed more important than us hanging out in the present. There were even multiple times when one of my friends asked another person at the table a question, and the other person responded without even lifting their head up from their phone.

How had I not noticed this sooner? There's a fairly easy answer: because it seemed *normal*.

People are on their phones a lot, and to fill the silence when a conversation lulled, pulling out our phones to check it seems like a habit.

But in seeing it first-hand from the outside that night, I could now see how much of a grip technology had on my friends and me. It was like watching Frodo with the ring in his pocket during *Lord of the Rings*. The phone in my pocket was tempting me to use it even while I was with my friends.

According to a study conducted by LivePerson, the leading provider of cloud mobile and online business messaging solutions, 65 percent of the four thousand participants in the study stated they communicate with others digitally more frequently than in person. This number increased specifically for Gen Z members in the US with 73.7 percent of the respondents relying more on digital communication than in person.

Not only that, but traditional norms which occurred prior to the beginning of Gen Z in 1995 are slowly changing as well. The 41.6 percent of the Gen Z respondents in the study consider it acceptable to text at a family dinner, and 27.7 percent of the respondents think it's acceptable to text in the middle of an in-person conversation.[57]

Former Harvard basketball player Henry Welsh said, "Today we have an endless stream of content at the wave of a finger that people didn't have access to 20 years ago. There's so much content to sift through out there from podcasts,

---

57   LivePerson, Inc., "Gen Z and Millennials Now More Likely to Communicate with Each Other Digitally than in Person," *PR Newswire*, October 17, 2017, accessed May 25, 2020.

to news, and I'm constantly checking updates for the latest segment. There are a lot of upsides to having a computer that can essentially fit into your palm, but everyone having a smartphone in their back pocket has become pervasive."

The *Nielsen Company's* 2017 study showed 45 percent of the Gen Z generation received a cellphone. In the study, 45 percent of Gen Z members in the US received a cellphone and mobile service plan between the ages of ten and twelve. Additional data from a study by the Center for Generational Kinetics the following year showed 25 percent of Gen Z had a smartphone before the age of ten while in elementary school.[58]

But technology has affected us in many more ways than just receiving a phone at a young age. There is an important psychological and social change which has occurred with this rise in technological advancement. In addition to the increase in Gen Z users of smartphones, an attachment has developed as well. This attachment to smartphones has resulted in 55 percent of Gen Z using their phones for five hours or more per day, according to the Center for Generational Kinetics article "How Obsessed is Gen Z with Mobile Technology?" The study goes a step further to say 31percent of Gen Z feels uncomfortable if they are without their phones for thirty minutes or more.[59]

This has resulted in an unfortunate trend for Gen Z. The constant attention and attraction to our cellphones and

---

58 "Mobile Kids: The Parent, the Child and the Smartphone," *Nielsen.com*, The Nielsen Company, February 28, 2017, accessed May 22, 2020.
59 Jared Boucher, "Top 10 Gen Z Statistics from 2018," The Center for Generational Kinetics, accessed May 23, 2020.

other electronics has had a detrimental psychological effect. It has decreased our in-person interactions with others and increased our loneliness.

According to a nationwide survey performed by global health service company Cigna, America is currently undergoing a "loneliness epidemic," with almost 50 percent of the study participants feeling lonely. Researchers surveyed more than twenty thousand adults aged eighteen and older and utilized the UCLA Loneliness Scale to tally scores on a scale of twenty to eighty, identifying those who scored above a forty-three as being officially lonely.

The study found the loneliness scores rose among the younger generations, with the youngest generation, Gen Z, feeling the loneliest. Gen Z scored a 48.3 overall. Millennials, those born between the years 1981 and 1996, scored a 45.3 on the loneliness scale. Gen X scored a dreary 45.1 and Baby Boomers scored a 42.4. Those of grandparenting or great-grandparenting age, the Greatest Generation, were the least lonely with a score of 38.6. Cigna's findings not only identified Gen Z (adults age eighteen to twenty-two) as the loneliest generation, but also the generation which claims to be in the worst health compared to other age demographics.[60]

University of Michigan graduate Drew Slipe commented on this saying, "It seems like everyone is always on their phones. It's a crutch. It should instead be about communicating with friends in a more genuine way."

---

60 Jena Hilliard, "New Study Reveals Gen Z as the Loneliest Generation in America," Addiction Center, last modified June 18, 2020, accessed May 20, 2020.

When I found this Cigna study, I was shocked. Technology's presence was the norm; I utilized the functions on my phone daily. As I got older, I hardly realized my cellphone use was increasing, and until the dinner with my friends, I didn't see the problem.

When I was in middle school, I heard one of my friend's parents say, "My life is on my phone." A phone appeared to be my extension to people and information from around the world, and it was empowering. Why not use it as much as I could?

Receiving my first cellphone when I was in sixth grade was a big step to becoming an adult and gaining responsibility. My parents wanted to reach me in case of an emergency, and a cell phone was the most practical way to accomplish this. If I went over to a friend's house, I could text to let them know, and I could give them a quick call if practice ran late.

To me, I thought getting a cellphone at that age was a rite of passage. My parents trusted me to be responsible and accountable for my whereabouts. But in addition, I now had a device all to myself I could now use in place of relying on my parents. My phone was a part of me, and I could use it in any way I pleased (within reason, because my parents still paid my phone bill).

My cellphone opened up so many possibilities in life. I could now play my music whenever, I could download the applications and games I wanted, and I could search for anything in the Safari browser. It was like a magic wand at my fingertips, and I had it in my pocket, close to me at all times. Each of my friends had cellphones, and I now had the ability to communicate with my friends through a few simple clicks on my cell phone keyboard. There was to be no more parents coordinating play dates.

Texting was so easy, and it allowed me to talk to multiple people at one time without seeing them in person. I could keep up relationships and talk to my friends who moved away or went to different schools. It allowed me to communicate effortlessly, but I noticed as I got into high school my phone use was bleeding into my relationships.

After seeing this in real life, I thought, "Have we truly become so consumed in a six-inch device in our pocket that we will tune out a person talking a foot away from us? Is face-to-face interaction soon becoming a thing of the past?"

My parents used to always say, "Phones away at the table," when we were eating dinner, but I never truly understood why until that summer night where I saw a dinner table full of my friends on their phones. It's not just phones that vie for the attention of Gen Z.

Even past communication on cell phones and laptops, technology has become an integral part of Gen Z entertainment today through *gaming*. A study conducted by the Nielsen Company showed sixty-six percent of Gen Z respondents listed gaming as their main hobby.[61]

---

61   Ryan Jenkins, "Who Is Generation Z? This Timeline Reveals It All," *Inc. com*, September 25, 2017, accessed May 22, 2020.

For Gen Z, Atari was a thing of the past. It was replaced by the Nintendo Game Cube and the XBOX, which were both released in 2001. Five years later, Nintendo developed the Wii as a fun way to exercise while gaming.

The sixty-six percent of Gen Z respondents in the Nielsen study means gaming ranked above playing outside and spending time with friends. These two staples of childhood are now taking a backseat to gaming.

I remember hearing growing up "Hey, let's play Call of Duty after school. We can go on Xbox Live." This meant each person on Xbox Live could play the same video game together from their respective houses without being under the same roof. Similar to texting, it presented the ability to play with friends who lived far away. But it bothered me I couldn't see my friends when we played.

Weather permitting, my idea of fun as a kid was running around and playing outside. My parents only allowed me to watch TV or play video games on the weekends, so I developed a sense of joy in playing outside rather than sitting on the couch inside. But as shown in the Nielsen study, I was in the minority of my fellow Gen Z peers.

Technology is an important part of the future success of Gen Z and of the total advancement of the human race. However, the correlation between the technological habits and the loneliness is alarming. This technological innovation should not come at the expense of human interaction.

Our in-person interactions are a break from technology, and Albert Einstein says, "it has become appallingly obvious that technology has exceeded our humanity." But, this doesn't have to be the case. University of Michigan graduate Will Minck told me while studying abroad in Barcelona, Spain he accidentally forgot to secure an international cell phone plan before he left. He went through his five-month study abroad experience as a "Wi-Fi nomad," only using his phone when he and his friends stopped somewhere with Wi-Fi, which was rare.

He said, "It was way easier to live in the moment. I appreciate all the conversations I had so much more, and I became more aware of my surroundings. I think my study abroad experience was enhanced by having limited use of my cellphone, and it gave me a whole new perspective on technology."

So some of my friends and I decided to try limiting our cell phone use. We started a routine where when we went out to eat, we all took our phones out of our pockets and placed them in a stack on the table. This way no one will be tempted to look at their screen while we're at dinner together and if someone did reach for their phone, the whole group would see it. A few times we even decided only one person would bring their phone when we went out in case of an emergency while the rest of the group left their phones at home.

Our phones are important to us and we need them for communication, but it's a balancing act with our social lives. The fact Gen Z's dependency on technology is causing loneliness is *scary*. We need to stop this trend now, but we need to first recognize there is a problem and a need for change.

It's simple. Our technology has become our *crutch*, so we just need to start walking on our own again without that crutch. We feel the need to pull our phones out during a silence in a conversation or when we wait in line or in an elevator around strangers. Our phones shouldn't be protection from others. That isn't their purpose. When that feeling creeps in of wanting to pull the phone out and escape from the present reality, instead talk to someone around you.

When we are with friends and family, our attention should go to the people around us instead of the screen in our pocket. Video games have become a popular hobby for our generation, which doesn't mean we neglect human interaction with our friends for screen time. Enjoying the company of those we care about is what we will remember years down the road, not beating a level or getting a special award for your avatar.

Technology will always continue to evolve. There will always be a new shinier product out on the market to catch our attention. It is up to us to recognize our human relationships trump our screens. Even Steve Jobs, the founder of *Apple*, recognized this. He said, "Technology is nothing. What's important is that you have faith in people, that they're basically good and smart, and if you give them tools, they'll do wonderful things with them." For my fellow members of Gen Z, we have the tools to make a lasting impact and leave this world better than when we inherited it, but we first have to believe in the power of humanity and look up from our screens.

CHAPTER 14

THE FOCUS IS ON MAKING A LIVING, BUT WE WANT TO MAKE A LIFE FOR OURSELVES

"I've learned that making a 'living' is not the same thing as 'making a life.'"

—MAYA ANGELOU

At parent-teacher conference nights in elementary school, I remember standing at my mom's side as she made small talk with the other classmates' parents. Inevitably, in every single conversation after pleasantries were exchanged between the parents, the same question came up: "So what do you do for a living?"

When I was younger, I noticed the question just seemed to be a part of the conversation whenever one adult met another. It was like a natural adult ritual when meeting another adult.

The answer to the question "What do you do for a living?" seemed to be a baseline for adults' first impressions of each other. Their careers were an extension of how others viewed them, and it was an important part of an adult's identity. How could I one day could give an answer which garnered a high level of respect and interest when I said what I did for a living?

Once I got to college, the prospect of laying the foundation for my career became more real. I was assigned a career college counselor, and I began to speak with her about how to apply to internships in the fields I was interested in. She had me look at jobs, their starting salaries, and how I could advance my career in different professions. I was excited to become a working member of society and find a career I was passionate about upon graduation.

I graduated college virtually in May 2020 in the middle of the COVID-19 pandemic. My future plans as well as those of my fellow members of Gen Z have been put on hold. My home state of California has been under safer-at-home guidelines since March 19, and all US states and territories received a federal disaster declaration. For my fellow members of Gen Z, many of us have ended the school year with online classes, and the class of 2020 has had our commencements either postponed or moved to a virtual format. This is not the ending any of us envisioned as a true send off from our respective institutions.

This has directly impacted many members of Gen Z including Drew Slipe, a University of Michigan graduate. He said, "I was in the final round of interviews for a job I wanted, and my hiring process was frozen. I didn't have a choice and with COVID-19, there were really no places hiring. I want to find a job that makes me happy and a place where I could fit in and be a part of a great business. But it's hard now."

My friends and fellow members of Gen Z, we've now had to adjust our vision of a future career due to COVID-19. I knew I wanted it, but now a successful career, like happiness, became even more difficult to envision in our immediate future.

Money and what most people perceive as "success" seemed to go hand-in-hand, yet I found it interesting there is no baseline for happiness saying if a person makes this amount of money, they are considered by society to be successful.

As a young kid in elementary school, I was told learning the material and working hard would prepare me for middle school. Middle school would prepare me for high school. High school would prepare me for college. College would prepare me for graduate school or a job. My parents, teachers, and coaches told me the ultimate goal in all the learning and hard work was to have a *successful career* one day.

University of Alabama graduate Tommy Von Der Ahe added, "Your whole life and for four years straight in college, you're told that if you get good grades and get your degree, you can have a fruitful career. But now with COVID-19, I have to adjust my future plans, and I know everyone else is doing the same. We're all just trying to figure out what the next best move is."

I heard the phrase repeated frequently growing up. My elementary school teachers and coaches would motivate me by saying, "If you put the effort in, you can be successful." My parents said if I got good grades, did well in sports, ate all my vegetables and drank my milk, I could be successful later in life. I listened because I wanted to reach that goal of having a successful career, even though I didn't quite know what it would look like.

But it was hard to imagine what a successful career looked like in my future. I knew I wanted success in life, so I tried to focus on learning in school and getting good grades as a step toward success. Because if I did well in school, I would be in the best position to get the successful career I wanted. I thought if I set a path through my major in college and prepared for a career by earning internships and working my way to the top, it would be my ticket. At least, that's what the adults told me.

However, for my fellow Gen Z members, this idea of finding a job out of college and having a successful career is a significant part of our identity. Gen Z, according to the Center for Generational Kinetics (the top Gen Z and millennial speaking, research and consulting firm), want jobs that do more than pay the rent. They want jobs which are emotionally fulfilling and intellectually stimulating.[62]

The idea of success is notably a large part of the Gen Z identity. Barna Group, a research and resource company located

---

62 Team CGK, "Generation Z Wants a Job," The Center for Generational Kinetics, accessed May 29, 2020.

in Ventura, California conducted two nationally representative studies through 2016 and 2017. The first study in 2016 included 1,490 US teenagers thirteen to eighteen years old, while the second study in 2017 included 507 US teenagers of the same ages. The researchers asked the participants to fill in the blank to complete this phrase, "My _____ is very important to my sense of self."

The results showed personal achievement, whether educational or professional (43 percent) was the highest rated response for what concept was most central to Gen Z's identity. The researchers at Barna Group conducted the same study with members of Gen X, Baby Boomers, and millennials, asking them to fill in the blank for the same phrase.

Comparing the results from the Gen Z study to those of the other generations, the researchers found Gen Z was 7 to 8 percent higher on their personal achievement response than millennials (35 percent) and nearly twice that of Baby Boomers (22 percent) and Gen X (21 percent).[63]

Additionally, according to 2019 data from *Entrepreneur.com,* 41 percent of Gen Z members plan to start their own business. Gen Z is passing millennials as the "entrepreneurial generation," and when asked what's important to them in their future careers, 64 percent of Gen Zers responded "inspiring work" was one of their top priorities.[64]

---

63 "Gen Z and Morality: What Teens Believe (So Far)," Barna Group, October 9, 2018, accessed May 30, 2020.

64 Entrepreneur Staff,"41 Percent of Gen Z-ers Plan to Become Entrepreneurs (Infographic)," *Entrepreneur*, Entrepreneur Media, January 15, 2019, accessed June 2, 2020.

Former Seattle University baseball player Tyler Yeh said, "Once you're out of college, you're on your own. Parents aren't there to help you as much, and your success in life is up to you. With any job market, there's never really a roadmap or path that lights up to tell you where to go with your career. But with this job market, it's really intimidating to think about success when all you're hearing about is people getting laid off."

Girls With Impact, a Connecticut based young female entrepreneurship initiative, conducted a 2019 study with five hundred Gen Zers which further confirmed the Gen Z desire to make a positive change through their careers. They found 65 percent of Gen Z respondents said they want to "create something world-changing," and another 44 percent said they expect to be the leader of their company during their career. But here's the kicker... 65 percent of the Gen Z respondents, the same percentage which said they want to create something world-changing, *expect to be happy in the workplace.*[65]

In the same study, the respondents listed their top priorities as: Being successful, getting a job, and having sound mental health.

Personal success and a fulfilling career are strong pillars of our Gen Z identity, but the current job market has made it increasingly difficult to turn our visions into reality. As we graduate college and graduate school in 2020, our promise of starting a career after school has been put on hold. How

---

65   Mark C. Perna, "Gen Z Wants To Change The World— At Your Company," *Forbes*, Forbes Media, December 19, 2019, accessed June 1, 2020.

can we achieve all three of those priorities of being successful, finding a job, and having sound mental health?

As we enter the job market, we must hold onto the desire to make a positive change through our careers. We all have unique passions and talents which make us unique as a generation. Yes, our expectations to get a job in a career we are interested in has now become harder to realize.

But so what!

Life doesn't give participation trophies. If we want to have successful careers, it starts with an unrelenting desire and a refusal to accept anything different will happen. One of my mentors, Tye Gonser told me, "success is different from happiness." He said, "Success is how others see you, happiness is how you see it for yourself. Out of college, you're still trying to figure out who you are as a person, but you slowly learn to what you care about and why. That's when you get true fulfillment."

Right now, we have a choice. We can give in to the negativity brought into our lives by the diminishing job market and we can feel sorry for ourselves. Or we can use our perspective to take us one step closer to our goals. As author and speaker Mark Desvaux says, "Some people see the glass half full. Others see the glass half empty. The enlightened are simply grateful to have a glass."[66]

---

66 Rania Merchak Andraos, "Looking at the Glass Half Full in the Translation Business," *TransPremium.com* (blog), TransPremium Translation, August 25, 2015, accessed June 1, 2020.

Well it may not be as pristine and ornate as we had imagined, we still have a glass waiting to be filled. We still have the opportunity to make an impact on this world, even if there are more doors closing in our faces than ones opening up. Now, it is critically important we focus on cultivating our happiness fingerprint and creating it in the world.

We have a long and difficult road and I won't sugarcoat the challenges ahead as a generation. Another one of my mentors, Jordan Matthews, said our success and failure go hand-in-hand in life, and those who find the success are the ones who aren't afraid to fail. He said, "I love what I do, and I don't just want to do it, I want to be great and leave a legacy. It's one thing to want a successful career when you're young, but are you willing to continue to push through the failures that you thought would be successes? You want to do something great? Then never lose that desire to be great no matter what comes up." Success is not free, and nothing will be handed to us.

Talking to Jordan inspired me and reminded me of a Winston Churchill quote I had heard years ago. He said, "Success is the ability to go from failure to failure without losing your enthusiasm."

Remember what we're trying to do is hard—we're trying to change the world! If we are struggling to find a job right now and our career plans have been thrown off course, that does not mean it's over. Similarly, it is not an excuse to give up.

Motivational speaker Rich Keller told me up until we graduate from college, we have a roadmap to follow from one grade to the next, but once we graduate, it's open road. He said,

"We feel like we need to get a job and a title because it will look the best to everyone else. You may get Superbowl tickets because of work. You got those tickets because of your job not because of who you are as a person. So we put so much value into what we do for work when instead we should be focusing on what we're passionate about."

We can channel our energy into creating good in our lives and in the world. Our career (or lack thereof right now) does not define us. Instead of seeing how others will view our career, we can view our work in terms of our passion and personal success in doing whatever we can to do a little bit of good each day.

The mark of our success will not be on our careers and in our salaries. When future generations look back at Gen Z, they will look at what we have done to make the world a better place. On our headstones, it won't talk about our careers, it will talk about what we meant to the people who loved us. Our humanity goes so far past what we "do for a living." Just as Maya Angelou says, for my fellow members of Gen Z, we should today and every day in our future focus on "making a life" rather than "making a living."

CHAPTER 15

THE "WHAT" AND THE "HOW" SET OUR PATH, BUT THE "WHY" MAKES IT UNIQUE

———

"He who has a why to live for can bear almost any how."
—FRIEDRICH NIETZSCHE

Why was my favorite word as a kid. That one word was my key to unlocking endless information. It was like a secret password to a vault of the world's information.

I loved asking "why" and stoking the flame of my curiosity, but looking back, my parents were probably frequently annoyed by this habit. So it would make sense when I asked a lot of my "why" questions, I would get a "because that's the way it is" from my parents.

It turns out this is completely normal, and there is actually a reason behind children asking "why." A 2009 study, which appeared in an issue of the journal *Child Development*, conducted by researchers at the University of Michigan discovered an important find which has influenced the last decade of child psychology.

The researchers used two separate studies of children ages two to five to focus on their "how" and "why" questions, in addition to their requests for explanatory information. In the first of the two studies, the researchers "examined longitudinal transcripts of six children's everyday conversations with parents, siblings, and visitors at home from ages 2 to 4." In the second study, they looked at "the laboratory-based conversations of 42 preschoolers, using toys, storybooks, and videos to prompt the children, ages 3 to 5, to ask questions."

The researchers focused on how the children reacted to the answers they received to their "why" questions and found the children seem to be more satisfied when they receive an explanatory answer compared to when they do not. In both studies, when the young children got an explanation they seemed satisfied, but when they got nonexplanatory answers like "because that's the way it is," they seemed dissatisfied and "were more likely to repeat their original question or provide an alternative explanation."

The data showed "examining conversational exchanges, and in particular children's reactions to the different types of information they get from adults in response to their own requests, confirms that young children are motivated to actively seek explanations," according to the University of

Michigan researchers. Additionally, the data showed the children "use specific conversational strategies to obtain that information. When preschoolers ask 'why' questions, they're not merely trying to prolong conversation, they're trying to get to the bottom of things."[67]

So there is a method to the madness of children constantly asking "why." But this word evolved as I got older. Instead of asking why something was the way it was, I began asking myself why I was doing what I was doing. Why did I want to play sports? Why did I choose my major? Why do I want to apply to this specific job? My "why" became almost like a way to screen my decision-making process. If I could satisfy myself with an answer for why I was doing something, I was probably doing the right thing.

This concept of having a "why" fascinated me, and while researching for a project in a college economics class I came across the work of best-selling author and motivational speaker Simon Sinek. Sinek first popularized the importance of "why" in his first TEDx Talk in 2009. He developed the Golden Circle Diagram as a visual representation of how the "what," "how," and "why" manifest themselves in reality. Sinek uses the Golden Circle Diagram, which is backed by biology and composed of three circles, to inspired leaders and organizations, regardless of size and industry, to think and communicate from the inside out rather than the outside in.[68]

67 Carolyn Gregoire, "How Being An Oldest, Middle Or Youngest Child Shapes Your Personality," *HuffPost Science*, last modified May 15, 2015, accessed May 27, 2020.

68 Simon Sinek, "How Great Leaders Inspire Action," TEDx Puget Sound, last modified September 2009, accessed May 29, 2020.

The outer circle represents "what," the second circle is "how," and the core represents "why." With regards to business, the "what" is the products or services a company sells. Every organization knows what they are selling or what they are buying.

Next, the "how" is the explanation of how a business does their work differently from other businesses in their field. The "how" is what makes the company unique and stand out to the consumer.

Finally, the "why" at the core of the Golden Circle Diagram is the belief of a company. The "why" is what drives and inspires the company to do business in the first place.

Sinek says the "why" is "never to make a profit. That is always a result." He further explains the "why" by saying "What's your purpose? What's your cause? What's your belief? Why does your organization get out of bed in the morning? And why should anyone care?" He says, "Very few organizations really know this."

As a result, the way companies communicate with their customers is from the outside in. They start with the clearest thing and end with the fuzziest thing. But according to Sinek, "inspired leaders and organizations, regardless of size and industry, think, act, and communicate from the inside out."

I thought about how I could apply Sinek's Golden Circle Diagram to my life and my personal motivation. I struggled to determine exactly what my "why" was, and I decided to ask a few of my fellow coworkers a few years older than me how his "why" has evolved since joining the workforce.

Associate attorney Bryan Bitzer said, "I've always thought of my 'why' under the umbrella of helping others, and that started for me as a kid. Both my parents worked in health care, and I saw how they used the strengths and tools to bring about change. Throughout high school and college, I recognized what I was good at and cultivated that over time to pursue my 'why'. But you have to translate that into action, and when every day is a grind and an ever-continuing wave, your 'why' has to be powerful enough to push through that difficulty."

I started to seriously think about my "why" during college, both as a student and an athlete. I looked at my personal motivation for playing collegiate baseball and why I wanted to go to law school. I played baseball because I loved the game and I loved being competitive. The subject matter in law school piqued my interest and gave me a way I could continue to cultivate my competitive nature.

I knew in my career I wanted to be doing work where I could help people, and I knew a juris doctorate degree would give me an effective foundation to do so. I wanted to know I made a positive difference in as many people's lives as possible.

However, growing up in Los Angeles I was surrounded by the entertainment industry. I would see celebrities when I went out to dinner, to a sports game, or even on a hike. I wanted the same level of fame and for people to recognize my face and name along with my future high-powered celebrity clients. I wanted to find a way to *matter* and to leave my legacy by any means necessary. I was obsessed.

As a member of Gen Z, we grew up watching celebrities and athletes entertain us on TV, and I wanted to be just like them. Former all-American water polo player and Brown University graduate Armen Deirmenjian said, "We see celebrities when we're kids, and we want to be just like them. If Lebron James is wearing a pair of shoes, then you want to be like Lebron when you play basketball, so you buy the shoes. But as I've gotten older, I've realized that's not what a job should be about. It's not about how big your wallet is; it's about seeing the change you can make."

In 2007, researcher Yalda T. Uhls conducted a study with Dr. Patricia Greenfield at the University of California, Los Angeles campus of the Children's Digital Media Center@LA on how Gen Z children viewed celebrities and fame. The researchers looked at sixteen different values communicated to Gen Z from their top TV shows in order of importance (one being the most important and sixteen being the least important). This study had been in place since the 1960s, and in every other decade, from the 1960s to the 1990s, *fame* ranked at the bottom of the list while *community feeling* (acceptance within a group) finished first or second in every previous year of the study.[69]

However, a major shift occurred in 2007 as "fame" took the top spot on the list of sixteen values after being ranked the least important last or close to last in every other decade. The study found in 2007, "fame was the number one value

---

69   University of California Los Angeles, "Popular TV Shows Teach Children Fame Is Most Important Value, Psychologists Report; Being Kind to Others Fell Dramatically in Importance over 10 Years," ScienceDaily, July 22, 2011, accessed June 3, 2020.

communicated to preteens on popular TV." Coincidentally, reality TV shows such as "Keeping Up with the Kardashians" became among the top TV shows for Gen Z, and Uhls and Greenfield ultimately came to the conclusion "in the 21st century, television influences children more than at any other point in its history."

This continued into an international trend as well for the young members of Gen Z. According to the *Daily Mail*, in 2009 a study was conducted in the United Kingdom where researchers asked children what they wanted to be when they grew up. The top three choices were sports star, pop star, or actor.[70]

After reading this I remembered a quote from famous actor and comedian Bill Murray: "I always want to say to people who want to be rich and famous: 'try being rich first'. See if that doesn't cover most of it. There's not much downside to being rich, other than paying taxes and having your relatives ask you for money. But when you become famous, you end up with a 24-hour job."

For a long time, I thought this was my "why." I wanted to be famous and become a household name. Why did I want this?

Because that's what I thought society valued most. The celebrities and athletes get the most attention, media coverage, and their lives looked amazing.

---

70   Michael Smith, "Studies Show That Children Just Want to Be Famous," Guardian Liberty Voice, Guardian Liberty Voice, August 3, 2013, accessed June 3, 2020.

But after working full-time as an executive assistant at a law firm in Los Angeles during my senior year of college, there was a moment with my mentor and partner at the firm, Tye Gonser, which changed my perspective. I realized that's not actually what I wanted, and wanting to be famous wasn't actually my "why."

One day as we both prepared our lunches in the kitchen, Tye asked me why I was going to law school. I had already gone through the application process and was accepted to multiple schools at this point, but I described to him my ambition and my desire to be successful and to be recognized.

He said, "Well what's your 'why?'" I fumbled through a response, and he said, "That's not your 'why'. Your 'why' is your motivation for doing something and how you can make a difference in the world. How will your 'why' affect other people? It's easy to say what you want, but you need to figure out what you can give to others first."

I understood what he was saying, but I had trouble putting my "why" into words. They were in my head, but when they reached my tongue they didn't come out the way I wanted them to. I knew I wanted to help people, but I had trouble understanding what I could give at my young age.

Weeks later my dad asked me the same question, but he put it a different way. Tying into what my "why" is, my dad asked me, "How can you use the skills you have to make a difference? Anyone can say they want to help people. How will you be different?" In using both Tye's and my dad's prompting, I wanted to really think about what my answers would be.

I thought about how I could help people using my voice, and I started really simple. University of Alabama graduate Tommy Von Der Ahe said, "My brother Matthew always puts things in perspective for me. He has Down Syndrome, but he wakes up every day and treats that day like a new adventure. He sees the good in the world and in people, and I want to embody that. When I look at my career, that is my reminder to do something meaningful past just a paycheck."

Every day, I wanted to make one person's day better in some way. Whether it was telling my mom a dumb joke to make her smile or even saying "hi" to a stranger on the street, I focused on the little things I could do to help those around me.

This made me feel good, and as I thought about my future, I wanted to emulate my ability to help people on a larger scale. I think I understand now what people mean when they say, "I do meaningful work." Wanting to be famous and a recognizable name only benefitted me and no one else. I was only thinking about how I would be perceived by others. Instead, my "why" turned into me wanting to give other members of my generation an opportunity to see a new perspective on different aspects of their lives and understand happiness, positivity, and optimism in a more holistic way.

When we choose our career path, we are making the conscious decision to engage in our "what." As we seek to differentiate ourselves in our respective field, we are cultivating our "how." But it is our "why" where we truly leave our impact. The meaningful change we want to create and the legacy we want to leave begins with our "why." It is past a salary and past a status symbol; it is why we want to put a smile on someone's face and bring positivity to the world. In fifty years, when someone asks us *why* we chose our career and *why* we made the choices we did, what will we tell them?

CHAPTER 16

RIDE THAT WAVE, BUT FIND THAT REFERENCE POINT

___

"No finite point has meaning without an infinite reference point."

—FRIEDRICH NIETZSCHE

"Reach for the stars and always chase your dreams because anything is possible." This is a seemingly powerful and impactful thing to say to a young kid, but what does this really mean? Is it just one of those lines adults say to kids to get them excited about their futures?

I heard this from my parents, teachers, and coaches when I talked to them about what I wanted to be in life, and I saw this theme pop up in every Disney movie I watched. Aladdin would stop at nothing to be a prince with Princess Jasmine, Pinocchio would not give up until he became a real boy, and Mulan defied her family and culture to become a warrior and defend her home. So I believed I could do whatever I set my mind to because I loved the idea I could make my dreams a reality and be something great.

Not once did I hear as a kid "be realistic" or "only shoot as high as you think you can go." Additionally, I didn't understand or even know about the concept of a *reference point*. I didn't have a standard for evaluating my future plans because I wanted to be a professional athlete more than anything when I was a kid, and most importantly, I really believed I could be one.

In seventh grade, during a school-wide career aptitude test, I remember bringing the test up to the teacher and asking why being a professional athlete wasn't an option to circle for "desired job." He told me the chances of becoming a professional athlete were so minuscule it would be unrealistic to list it as a viable career option to put on the aptitude test.

I came home from school so upset because my dream was deemed "unrealistic." What happened to "reach for the stars?" It seemed like there should be fine print or an asterisk somewhere saying, "but make sure it's realistically achievable." Without a reference point for the conceptualization of my future goals, anything less than realizing my dream was a failure. It was the best or bust.

This idea specifically came to light during a club baseball tournament when I was twelve. My team made it to the championship game of the large tournament, and we had played extremely well leading up to this final game. After going up to an early lead, we eventually lost by one run in heartbreaking fashion in the last inning.

After the game, there was a trophy ceremony where our coach was handed a second-place trophy and we were given medals and "runner-Up" t-shirts. As we cleaned up our dugout, I noticed one of my teammates throwing the shirt in the trashcan at the end of the dugout. As we walked toward our parents in the stands, I asked him why he did that. He responded second place doesn't deserve an award because it's nothing to be proud of. If he had brought it home, he would've burned it rather than keep it as a reminder.

This moment has always stuck with me. I hated to lose, and my friend reminded me second place is just the first loser. I was told to reach for the stars when I was young, and first place and being the best was the only thing which could satisfy that. Anything less was a disappointment. But former collegiate soccer player Kylee MacArthur brought a new perspective as she said, "When I was playing sports, it was all about constantly achieving and resetting my goals. You and your teammates can play the best game ever and still lose, and I learned to have my love for the game be my reference point regardless of the outcome."

I took this idea into my psychological research for this book, and I found a concept directly connected to the idea of a reference point for future goals. When we imagine "what could have been" after experiencing the negative outcome of an event, it is called *counterfactual thinking*. Thomas Gilovich, Scott F. Madey, and Victoria Husted Medvec from the Department of Psychology at Cornell University published a 1995 article, "When less is more: Counterfactual thinking and satisfaction among Olympic medalists" in the *Journal of Personality and Social Psychology*.[71]

In the study, the researchers coded the facial expressions of Olympic medalists and found something very interesting. As expected, the gold medalists exhibited the most joy and most visibly happy facial expression. However, the researchers found bronze medalists showed more positive emotional expressions than the silver medalists.

The silver medalist had just become the second best in the entire world in their sport and had outperformed the bronze medalist, yet their facial expressions looked as if they had lost. The researchers concluded this was due to the feeling of being so close to the gold, which diminished the joy of winning a silver medal.

In that moment, the reference point for silver medalists was surrounding what more they could have done to earn the gold, not having achieved the silver medal. Contrastingly, the researchers also concluded the bronze medalists were less likely to focus on how their performance could have been better to win the silver medal. Instead, the bronze medalists appeared happier and exhibited more visibly positive facial expressions because they likely focused on not receiving a medal and had not slipped to fourth place. Where the silver medalists lamented what they had missed out on, the bronze

---

71 T. Gilovich Medvec, V.H. Madey, and S.F. Gilovich, "When Less Is More: Counterfactual Thinking and Satisfaction among Olympic Medalists," *Journal of Personality and Social Psychology*, 69, no 4 (October 1995): 603-10.

medalists found solace in knowing they will forever go down in history as an Olympic medalist.

I saw this first-hand during the 2018 Winter Olympics. While watching highlights on ESPN, I saw the US women's hockey team had shocked 3-2 with a shootout win over Canada to bring home the gold medal. However, that wasn't the headline of the segment. The headline was "Canada's Jocelyne Larocque apologizes for taking off silver medal after loss to US." Star defenseman Jocelyn Larocque had taken off her silver medal seconds after the official put it around her neck and refused to put it back on despite pleas from her teammates and jeers from the crowd.[72]

The world heavily criticized Larocque for poor sportsmanship. Larocque exemplified what the 1995 study found, and in her apology Larocque admitted the wave of emotions from being so close to the gold and not obtaining it got the best of her in the moment.

I wanted my reference point to encompass happiness and passion instead of solely focusing on achieving my goal. Former all-American water polo player at Brown University Armen Deirmenjian said, "As an athlete in a team sport, it's easy to look ahead in a tournament or in a season to where you want to be in the end. But I know I always felt better winning that bronze as opposed to losing in the finals because the team ends on a win. If you're always focused on winning the championship or being named the MVP, you miss out on the

---

72   Gutting, Casey, Yahoo! Sports. February 22, 2018. accessed Apr. 19, 2020. Hhttps://sports.yahoo.com/usa-wins-hockey-gold-canadian-player-promptly-removes-silver-medal-presentation-081201056.html.

happiness that comes along with playing." But this was hard because I still just wanted to be the best. In everything in life, I had always held myself to the highest possible standard, and when I didn't achieve my goal, I thought it was because I didn't work hard enough.

This vicious cycle never really allowed me to feel proud of my accomplishments because of my reference point. My happiness was based on the achievement of my ultimate dream of being a professional athlete and grabbing the star I had been reaching for my whole life. However, through multiple serious injuries in high school and college, I realized my body couldn't support this dream. I would not become a professional athlete, and now I was left without an identity.

I wanted to cultivate a new reference point and find a new dream, but I felt like I was trying to hit a target from fifty yards away while blindfolded and on horseback. What will I do? How can I just be happy?

As I pondered these questions, I came across a very interesting story in a video by motivational speaker and author Jay Shetty. The story is about an elementary school teacher assigning a simple task to her young students: write down what you want to be in life.[73]

That night after class, the teacher reviewed the variety of answers her students put on the index cards. She came across a variety of dream occupations, including astronaut, actor,

73   Jay Shetty, "Redefining Happiness: Street Philosophy with Jay Shetty," *HuffPost*, September 15, 2016, accessed Mar. 16, 2020.

scientist, and president thrown in the mix. However, there was one answer that stood out to the teacher amongst the rest.

After class the next day, the teacher asked the young boy to stay after to talk to him about his answer. As his answer to the teachers prompt in class the day before, the young boy wrote one word on the index card: *happy*. The teacher tells the child she was looking for what the child wanted to be in life occupation-wise. The teacher ends by saying to the boy, "I think you misunderstood the assignment."

The young boy looked the teacher in the eye and respectfully answered, "No ma'am. *I think you misunderstood life.*"

When I first heard this story it amazed me, and I had to listen to it one more time to let the boy's response sink in. That boy could have joined his classmates and said any of the dream jobs the average nine-year-old would like, but he didn't.

Instead of responding with a job he wanted, the young boy set his reference point at his own personal happiness.

I could say with 100 percent confidence if someone had asked me when I was younger what I wanted to be when I grew up in one word, the word "happy" would not have crossed my mind in a million years. I think professional athlete, treasure hunter, musician, and movie star would have come to the forefront of my mind long before "happy."

For our reference points in life, it all comes down to our perspective and how we conceptualize our goals. As we transition from college into the real world, we all have personal and professional goals and places we want to get to in life. However, in our pursuit of these goals, let's think about them in a different way than "reaching for the stars."

If we "reach for the stars" and we don't attain those lofty goals, it is a crushing realization as we hurdle back down to reality.

Instead of this phrase, I decided to create one of my own: *ride your wave.*

With this phrase, our wave is unique to us, and it is our responsibility to ride it in the way we see fit. We are not reaching to attain something far off in the distance with the possibility of falling back to Earth when our dream doesn't come true. Associate account strategist at Google Owen Rothman echoed this idea in his life saying, "Reaching for the stars is really a Catch 22 because you are always reaching for something that won't ever leave you feeling fulfilled and satisfied. Everyone has their board in the ocean catching their wave, and inherently some will catch bigger waves than others and stay on their boards longer. You just need to focus on riding your wave without hopping on other peoples."

If our wave crashes, we paddle out and find another one. Because our goals are attainable and realistic, this phrase brings more flexibility to our psyche than "reach for the stars "and "chase your dreams."

It's so easy to focus on what we didn't do, what we could have done, or what we didn't achieve. It's logical to think about what could have been. But this only makes us miserable.

Constantly focusing on what didn't happen and what we wished was different serves no productive purpose.

Life is only moving forward, and there will always be another wave. When we fall off a wave we so badly wanted or we even missed the chance to catch the wave we thought was meant for us, good news: *another one will come.* Like the ocean flowing toward the sand, our lives will continue on. We as a generation need to understand for us to accomplish our goals, we first need to solidify our reference point of catching our wave.

We cannot lament over how the challenges in our personal and professional lives have affected our goals. Every generation before us has faced challenges. The achievement of our goals begins with our ownership of our wave, our willingness to ride it for as long as we can, and our determination to paddle back out when we fall off our board. If we incorporate happiness into our reference points, we will be able to ride our waves for a long time.

My fellow members of Gen Z, let's be like the bronze medalist and realize our accomplishments are to be celebrated through our reference points. Each wave is an opportunity to achieve our goals, and with our reference points as our anchor and happiness as our barometer, our goals are attainable. The events of yesterday do not define our ability to accomplish our goals tomorrow, and the last wave we attempted to ride has no bearing on our upcoming wave. When we do achieve our goals and ride our wave, we will look back to this moment and see our reference point spurred our desire to create meaningful change.

CHAPTER 17

REALITY MAY SEEM FINITE, BUT OUR IMAGINATION IS MORE POWERFUL THAN WE KNOW

———

"Imagination is the beginning of creation. You imagine what you desire, you will what you imagine, and at least, you create what you will."

—GEORGE BERNARD SHAW

It was a hot summer day, and sweat poured down my face. I could feel the burning in my legs and lungs growing stronger with every step. My coach yelled from the endzone, "Go to your happy place in your mind. Block out the pain!" I tried to "think happy thoughts" and imagine I was somewhere way better than on the field in the scorching summer sun to lessen the pain.

I tried to imagine myself walking on the beach with the sand in between my toes instead of running in between the dashes on the field with little black AstroTurf pellets popping up as I ran. I tried to picture a blood-orange sunset slowly cascading down the horizon line until just barely peeking out above the ocean instead of the heat waves I saw ahead of me on the turf. I did everything I could to place myself on a beach in my head and leave the turf field I was currently on. By focusing on the image in my head, maybe I could trick my body into not focusing on the burning in my legs and the dryness in my mouth as I breathed in hot summer air.

Beginning around the 1920s, "a vast literature began to emerge that stressed simultaneously the importance of being happy, the personal responsibility to gain happiness, and the methods available" in the United States. Specifically, the concept of a "happy place" began to captivate psychologists, and the research on its ability to help us cope with stressful or threatening situations has been developed by psychologists throughout the twentieth century.[74]

Notably, Joel Pearson, a psychologist and neuroscientist at the University of New South Wales in Sydney, Australia, and his colleagues found in a 2011 study our evaluation of our mental imagery shares a direct correlation with our subsequent performance on cognitive tasks in reality.[75]

---

74 Peter N Stearns, "The History of Happiness," *Harvard Business Review,* October 8, 2014, accessed June 2, 2020.

75 Rebecca Keogh and Joel Pearson, "Mental Imagery and Visual Working Memory," PLOS ONE, December 14, 2011, accessed June 2, 2020.

In a trying scenario, focusing our brains on a mental image separate from the discomfort or pain we're enduring in the present allows us to better cope with the situation. Whether it's a memory from the past or envisioning our ideal future, our "happy place" creates a mental baseline for happiness which we can draw from at any point in time.

I had always thought of my "happy place" as a tool to escape my current reality. No matter the situation, it was comforting knowing I could use my imagination to take my mind to something better. But when I came home from college to help care of my family, it was harder to escape my reality and imagine better times. I tried to think happy thoughts, but they didn't seem to make my reality easier to cope with.

It seemed unrealistic to think happy thoughts could translate into a happy reality. It couldn't be so *simple*. There had to be more to it.

According to the cosmic law of cause and effect, there will be an equal and opposite reaction for every action. The action of thinking creates the reaction of our brain telling our bodies to do or say something.

I remember when I was young and we were fishing, my dad would always say if I had negative thoughts, the fish could sense it and wouldn't bite. He said the fish could feel our energy on the boat and would only go near our bait if we had positive thoughts. So I would always try to think positive thoughts to attract the fish to my bait, but the fish would never bite whenever I actively tried to have these thoughts.

As I began my research on how to be happy again, I became interested in how to use my imagination to create my desired future. One of my first Google searches yielded a story based in the ancient Greek myth of Pygmalion and Galatea.

Pygmalion was a sculptor who was dedicated to his art and despised women so much he had vowed never to marry. One day, Pygmalion carved the statue of a woman of unparalleled beauty, and upon completing the statue fell madly in love with his creation.

He named his work Galatea, and every day Pygmalion stared at the statue and envisioned she would transform into a real woman. He imagined every night what it would be like to marry Galatea, which he was convinced would one day happen. The goddess of love, Aphrodite, was touched by Pygmalion's devotion and granted his wish of turning Galatea into a real woman. Pygmalion and Galatea fell madly in love and happily married soon after.

Although unrealistic, I was intrigued by Pygmalion's dedication to turning his imaginative thoughts into reality. What was I doing wrong when I wished for the fish to bite the hook when I was a kid, and why did Pygmalion get what he wished for when I didn't?

In searching for this answer, I came across a famous 1968 psychological experiment demonstrating the effects of a "self-fulfilling prophecy" conducted by Robert Rosenthal, a professor of social psychology at Harvard University, and his colleague Leonore Jacobson.[76]

Rosenthal and Jacobson gave a group of elementary school students an intelligence test and informed their teachers the results predicted their intellectual capacity. Rosenthal and Jacobson randomly selected a sample of 20 percent of the students in each class and told the professors and the selected students they had more significant potential for progress compared to the other students.

Eight months later, they gave the intelligence test to all the students. The 20 percent of students chosen, the experimental group, showed significant improvement on the test compared to the remaining students, the control group. Rosenthal and Jacobson concluded the students in the experimental group had improved more on the test because they believed they were rising to their potential. The positive expectations around them had a direct effect on their performance results, and these results became known as the Rosenthal effect or Pygmalion effect. The results explain the phenomenon of how expectations affect our performance and effect our self-esteem.

Fourteen years later in 1982, Rosenthal along with Israeli psychologists Alisha Y. Babad and Jacinto Inbar built on the research involved in the "Rosenthal Effect" by looking at how our own expectations for ourselves affect our performance. Rosenthal and his colleagues developed the Galatea effect,

---

76 "The Pygmalion Effect in the Classroom," *Philonotes. com*, PHILO, October 19, 2019, accessed June 1, 2020.

which suggests when we believe in our abilities to achieve a goal we'll be more likely to achieve it.[77]

Armed with this new knowledge, I revisited the question of why Pygmalion had been successful in his endeavor but I hadn't. As an eager ten-year-old sitting on the boat, gripping the gently bobbing rod tightly, I was thinking positive thoughts because I wanted to catch the fish. I wanted the result and the feeling of reeling it in, but I had no concrete vision of what it would look like. Pygmalion had envisioned Galatea as a real woman and visualized marrying her as opposed to simply wishing she would turn from stone to flesh.

But to begin planning out the application of visualization in my life, I tried to understand more at a neurological level how something from my brain could transfer over into reality. UC Berkeley graduate Chris Novia said, "Imagination is one of the greatest tools we have as human beings, and it's not just confined to our memories. Whenever I'm going through a tough time, I think about being on my surfboard at sunset or feeling the butterflies in my stomach before I start a race. In my mind, when I think about those things, I just feel better about what's happening in the moment."

In the *limbic system* in our brains, we have two very important parts of the brain performing essential functions: the *hippocampus* and the *amygdala*. The *hippocampus* converts our temporary memories into permanent ones to be stored

77   E.Y. Babad, J. Inbar, and R. Rosenthal, "Pygmalion, Galatea, and the Golem: Investigations of Biased and Unbiased Teachers," *APA PsychNet*, American Psychological Association, *Journal of Educational Psychology*, 74 volume 4: 459-474, accessed May 31, 2020.

within our brain, and the *amygdala* allows our bodies to respond to emotions, memories, and fear. As we take in the world around us, the electrical signaling of neurons in our brain flows from the *occipital lobe*, which controls our vision, to the *parietal lobe*, which controls our sensory comprehension. The flow of neurons indicates what we are experiencing is in fact our reality.

However, when the electrical signaling of neurons flow in the opposite direction from the parietal lobe up to the occipital lobe, what our brains see is *imaginary*. This is why we are able to imagine an event or conjure up an image we are not actually seeing in front of us at that given moment in reality.

Researchers at the Karolinska Institute in Sweden published a critically important neurological study in the scientific journal *Current Biology* in 2013. The study consisted of a series of experiments for ninety-six healthy volunteers. The researchers used illusions which altered the participants' sensory information by changing or distorting their visual and auditory perceptions. One of the experiments in the series consisted of participants experiencing the illusion of two passing objects colliding head on as opposed to passing each other when they imagined a sound at the moment the two objects hit.[78]

The results of this study showed neuronal signals created by imagined stimuli have the ability to integrate with signals generated by real stimuli of a separate sensory modality to

---

78 "Imagination Can Affect Sight, Sound Senses: Study," Majlis-e-Ulama-e-Shia (Europe), accessed May 31, 2020.

build robust multi-sensory precepts. This means our mind can actually play tricks on us by changing the illusions of what we think we hear and see.

Christopher Berger, a doctoral student at the Karolinska Institute's Department of Neuroscience and lead author of the study explained "what we imagine hearing can change what we actually see, and what we imagine seeing can change what we actually hear."

Translating these findings into reality, Chris Bergland is a personified example of the power of imagination and perception. He holds the Guinness World Record for running (153.76-miles in twenty-four hours on a treadmill) and completed the Triple Ironman (the longest nonstop triathlon in the world) with a record-breaking time of thirty-eight hours and forty-six minutes. In his book, *The Athlete's Way: Sweat and the Biology of Bliss*, Bergland shares how he was able to transcend physical discomfort as an Ironman triathlete and ultra-runner.

He said, "As an athlete, pain became a subjective experience that I could reframe as being a source of joy. Every 'sufferfest' genuinely became an ecstatic process while I was competing in ultra-endurance events. The ability to use my imagination to reshape perceptions of reality allowed me to win races. Anyone can use his or her imagination to overcome difficulty and achieve success in life and sport."[79]

---

79 Christopher Bergland, "Imagination Can Change Perceptions of Reality," *Psychology Today*, June 28, 2013, accessed June 1, 2020.

I asked current relief pitcher at the University of Michigan, Blake Beers, about the power of mental fortitude in collegiate sports. He said, "Sports constantly test your will to continue playing and your belief in your abilities. All that training, all the long mornings in the weight rooms and long nights at practice don't mean anything if your head isn't right when you step onto the field. I try my best to dedicate time before every game to visualize my success and make that hard work count when I step on the mound."

A few years after Karolinska Institute's study in 2018, researchers at the University of Colorado Boulder and Icahn School of Medicine conducted a critically important brain imaging study with sixty-eight healthy participants who were trained to associate a sound with an uncomfortable electric shock.[80]

This was the first neuroscience study to illustrate imagining a threat can actually alter the way it is represented in our brains. The researchers divided the participants into three groups and placed sensors on their skin to measure their bodily responses while also monitoring their brain activity through a functional magnetic resonance imaging (fMRI).

The first group was exposed to the threatening sound while the second group was asked to imagine the threatening sound. Both groups produced very similar results in both bodily response and brain activity with respect to a fear or aversion to the threatening sound. The two groups were repeatedly exposed to this sound, with the first group actually hearing

---

80   Lisa Marshall, "Your Brain on Imagination: It's a Lot like the Real Thing, Study Shows," *CU Boulder Today,* University of Colorado Boulder, December 6, 2018, accessed May 31, 2020.

it and the second group repeatedly imagining it, without any electrical shock.

During the later exposure to the sound, the researchers found the participants in these two groups experienced a process called *extinction,* where the sound which had previously induced fear no longer ignited the same response.

The third group was asked to imagine pleasant bird and rain sounds with no mention of any threatening sound. However, once exposed to the threatening sound, this group showed a different brain reaction. In going from the pleasant bird and rain sounds to the threatening sound, this group's fear response to the sound persisted. In the first two groups, the participants had overcome their fear through *extinction*, but the third group with the bird and rain sounds experienced prolonged fear.

This led the researchers to reconfigure how we perceive our fears and challenges from a neurological perspective. The study built on previous research which showed imagining an act can activate and strengthen regions of the brain involved in its real-life execution, which in turn improves our per-formance in reality. However, this study brings compelling evidence we have the ability to update the memories in our brains, inserting new details based on how we want to view the memory.

"If you have a memory that is no longer useful for you or is crippling you, you can use imagination to tap into it, change it and reconsolidate it, updating the way you think about and experience something," said Marianne Cumella Reddan, the lead author in the study who works in the Cognitive and Affective Neuroscience Lab at the University of Colorado Boulder. The researchers' findings in this study suggest imagination can be a powerful tool in helping people overcome their phobias and anxiety-related disorders.

Using our imaginations to combat anxiety is important because anxiety disorders are the most common mental illness in the US. Anxiety disorders affect forty million adults in the United States age eighteen and older, or 18.1 percent of the population every year, according to the Anxiety and Depression Association of America.[81]

For Gen Z, anxiety is a key issue. In a 2018 American Psychological Association study, 91 percent of Gen Z adults responded saying they felt physical or emotional symptoms, such as depression or anxiety, associated with stress.[82]

A 2018 study at the University of Illinois in Chicago (UIC) on the underlying causes of anxiety found increased sensitivity to uncertain threat or a fear of the unknown was the main source of anxiety. Research Assistant Professor of Psychiatry and Clinical Psychologist at the UIC College of Medicine Dr. Stephanie Gorka says this is called *anticipatory anxiety*. She says, "It could be something like not knowing exactly when your doctor will call with test results."[83]

---

81   "Facts & Statistics," Anxiety and Depression Association of America, accessed June 2, 2020.

82   Sophie Bethune, "Gen Z More Likely to Report Mental Health Concerns," *Monitor on Psychology*, American Psychological Association, 1 volume 50 (January 2019), accessed June 1, 2020.

83   Jeremy Dean, "One Personality Trait Is At The Heart Of Many Anxiety Disorders," *PsyBlog*, November 21, 2016, accessed June 3, 2020.

This anticipatory anxiety is born and bred in our minds similar to our imagination. However, trying to use our imagination as an "escape from reality" is limiting its capabilities. During a difficult time, trying to escape in our imagination is only putting a bandage on our wound. It may help get us through the time, but it won't actually change our reality.

Similarly, thinking happy thoughts is a good exercise, but the thoughts themselves won't change our reality either. Current Division I college baseball player at the University of Richmond, Dan Leckie said, "I try not to attach positivity or negativity to any outcome. Instead I look at the outcome for what it is, my reality. When you have that burning motivation to push toward your goals and you're truly grateful for what you have, then you will have less doubt and see that you can achieve them."

Instead of simply thinking positive thoughts, I now visualize my goals and dreams for where I want to get to in the future.

My imagination is no longer an escape; it is my motivation during difficult times. Instead of looking back on a happy memory from the past, I envision what I desire in a happy future. When I'm in the middle of a long night of studying or a grueling workout, instead of imagining I was somewhere else, I think about how my actions are a step toward the future I want.

As a generation, we cannot underestimate the effort required to achieve the success we envision, but it is important to first understand how to think about it. When we envision our goals, it doesn't mean we ignore the hard work necessary to reach them. It means we lean into hard work. In doing so, I switched my thinking from "I'm going to be the best and win," to "I'm going to take the time to put in the hard work to become the *best version of myself.*"

Additionally, our vision and goals cannot be solely reliant on our desired outcome. Our positivity isn't based off getting the reward of "winning" because our positive use of our imagination to realize our dream isn't contingent on winning or losing. We are making the conscious choice to envision our goals with positive direction right now.

I had the opportunity to speak with Jennifer Chaeng, the director of Digital Marketing at Mental Health America, one of the nation's leading nonprofit organizations committed to mental health advocacy and wellness. She said, "In stressful situations, human beings are more resilient than we realize, and in taking the time to work on our mental fortitude, we can train our brain to 'look for the good.' Be as kind to yourself as you would be to a friend and support yourself while you work to support others. The happiness and peace we desire starts with our effort in self-compassion and understanding more about how our mental state translates into our actions."

Building on Jennifer's point, our imagination and visualization are important for weathering the bumps in the road which will shake our energy bus as it moves toward our goals. If we are open to acknowledging these challenges and accept our desired future happiness is not simply something we can wish into reality, we can begin to lay our mental foundation with this understanding.

Since I was a kid, I've always had a tendency to look so far into the future I lose sight of the present. I could envision a happy future I wanted so badly, but didn't know what I could do in the present to begin making that future a reality.

So while working full-time at a law firm in Los Angeles and going to school full-time during my senior year of college, I began to do a short goal visualization each morning. I sat down on the floor next to my bed, read through my goals list, and closed my eyes. This even evolved into talking out loud and mimicking the physical motions of my goals as I envisioned them. Each day is an opportunity to get one step closer to realizing the future goals in our heads, and each day reminds us all to be grateful for the present.

By focusing on our present gratitude each day, we will use our imagination effectively and productively envision our desired futures. If we don't first believe we can attain our goals, others won't buy in either. It starts with us, and it starts between our ears.

Let's utilize the full power of our imaginations, and instead of escaping our reality, let's embrace it. Our goals will take dedication, commitment, and most importantly, time. In understanding how our thoughts can affect our reality, we will best seize the opportunities which will arise in our future.

CHAPTER 18

WE WANT TO CONFORM TO "BEING BUSY," BUT SOCIALIZATION IS OUR SOURCE OF HAPPINESS

———

"How did it get so late so soon? It's night before it's afternoon. December is here before it's June. My goodness how the time has flown. How did it get so late so soon?"

—DR. SUESS

It made absolutely no sense when I watched the clock during class. It literally never moved. Five minutes during the lecture seemed like a never-ending eternity. It didn't seem fair when I was on vacation with my family or spending time with my friends, time seemed to go by in the blink of an eye. As I got older and gained more responsibility, time became an increasingly precious commodity. There never seemed to be enough hours in the day to do everything on my list.

I thought being busy was the norm. If I was busy, it meant I was challenging myself, and to some extent, being productive in my work. I also felt a little pride in telling people, when they asked me how I'm doing, "I'm really busy. Got a lot going on!" Baylor University relief pitcher Daniel Caruso commented on staying busy in life saying, "There's so much pressure to be successful, so you end up wanting to do everything all the time in order to get that success. You want to satisfy your dreams as soon as possible and being busy is the way everyone thinks we need to get there. This gets overwhelming sometimes with so much going on all the time, but when I look around everyone's busy, so it makes me want to be busy too."

But this feeling is actually rooted in how Americans view being busy as a status symbol.

Silvia Bellezza, an associate professor of business in marketing at Columbia University, and her colleagues conducted a series of experiments in 2017 to analyze what psychologists call "status attribution"—characteristics helped an individual achieve a higher status in society.[84]

In the first experiment, Belleza and her team looked at 1,100 examples of online "humble bragging," analyzing posts with captions such as "I'm just so swamped with all my charity work." Many of the social media posts came from famous celebrities, and Belleza's team noticed the one common

---

84   Alan Mozes, "I'm Just Too Busy' — Is Being Overworked the New Status Symbol?" *Health Day News*, MedicineNet, Apr. 13, 2017, accessed June 4, 2020.

thread was "a tendency to complain about 'having no life' or 'being in desperate need for a vacation.'"

In their second experiment, Belleza's team asked their participants to say what their thoughts were when hearing the phrase "being busy." Belleza's team gave the options of spending a lot of time at work, spending a lot of time performing house-related chores, or spending a lot of time engaged with hobbies or leisure activities.

For their third experiment, Belleza's team recruited three hundred

men and women and asked them to guess the social status and wealth of a series of Facebook users who had recently posted on their timeline about leisure activities or being busy with work.

Belleza and her colleagues concluded from the results of all three experiments Americans viewed constantly working in a more favorable light than leisure seeking. Additionally, they found "being busy" is considered a status symbol for Americans and garners a higher status attribution than leisure seeking.

In the 1950s, social psychologist Solomon Asch conducted the famous "Line Experiment" in which he illustrated why human beings have a tendency to conform to the masses. He used 123 male college students and told them he was giving them a vision test, showing them a picture of a vertical line, followed by a series of different length lines, one of which was the same length as the original. Asch asked the participants to identify which line was the same length as the first line.[85]

However, he placed eleven participants who were instructed to purposely choose the wrong line and one participant who was given no instruction and was the actual subject in the experiment. The subject was placed at the far end of the group for certain questions, so they would be the final one to answer.

The results of the study showed the subject was more likely to give a false response after the other members of their group (the actors) purposely gave an incorrect response. The participant generally gave the correct answer when the other participants did not give a false answer. However, when the subject was the last in line and all other eleven participants gave the wrong answer, so did the subject.

Asch conducted interviews with the subjects and asked them to explain why they behave in this way. Many of the subjects admitted they changed their answers after hearing others in their group reply differently, and one even said, "...at times I had the feeling: 'to heck with it, I'll go along with the rest.'"

Belleza's research on "being busy" creating a status symbol in the US and Asch's research on conformity lend evidence to why Gen Z feels so busy and thinks that is normal. Dr. Laurie Santos, a professor of psychology at Yale University, discusses in her podcast "The Happiness Lab" how this sense

---

85   Saul McLeod, "Solomon Asch - Conformity Experiment," *Simply Psychology*, last modified December 28, 2018, accessed June 5, 2020.

of business is causing Gen Z to feel overwhelmed and has a negative effect on their health.

She says we experience what has been deemed by psychologists as "time famine," where we are essentially *starving* for more time, and this famished feeling has a significantly negative effect on our psyche. People who report feeling starved for time have a higher likelihood of reporting symptoms of anxiety, depression, and feeling holistically less happy than those who feel like they have lots of free time.

These people are deemed by psychologists as "time affluent" because they feel wealthy in time and experienced more prolonged periods of contentment compared to those starved for time. She goes on to say we have a tendency to misestimate how busy we actually are because our minds trick us into thinking we are incredibly busy all the time.

Dr. Santos drew on her own experience, saying she sometimes surprises her Yale students by cancelling class, and one students' reaction illuminated the importance of time affluence. Upon cancelling class, one of her students burst into tears. The girl told her it was the first time she had an hour off all semester, and she had almost forgotten what it was like to have some free time. Dr. Santos concluded by saying, "Adding even a few extra minutes to our perceived time banks can feel really good."[86]

---

86 "The Happiness Lab with Dr. Laurie Santos: For Whom the Alarm Clock Tolls," Pushkin Industries, Apple Podcasts, May 24, 2020, accessed June 6, 2020.

But it's hard to find these extra minutes when we're focused on "being busy" and pursuing our goals. Researchers at Savanta, a business-to-business marketing research company, executed a "Work-Life Balance" study in 2019 along with Priceline, surveying one thousand full-time working Americans. The researchers wanted to see how different generations viewed taking time off work.

Nearly a quarter (24 percent) of Gen Z in the study reported they felt guilty taking any time off work and did not use all or any of their vacation days. This was 5 percent higher than millennials (19 percent), 8 percent higher than Gen X (16 percent), and three times higher than Baby Boomers (8 percent).

An additional quarter (24 percent) of Gen Z in the study stated they worry about taking time off work because they feel people will judge them for doing so, and they feel they would be more successful if they decided to neglect their time off. The next closest generation which reported feeling the same in regards to taking time off was millennials at 15 percent.[87]

As I got older, I shared this feeling of not wanting to take breaks from my work or have a rest day during my week. If I was resting, I knew someone out there was outworking me, and I had this idea taking a break was detrimental to achieving success. I wanted to be as productive as possible with my time and this meant "being busy."

---

87 Gina Vaynshteyn, "Work Guilt' Is Real and It's Keeping You From Using Your Vacation Days," Priceline Press Center, October 28, 2019, accessed June 5, 2020.

But with this feeling of "being busy" came a feeling of FOMO (Fear of Missing Out), and I wondered how I could best use my time to fit everything I wanted to into my day.

In 2018 Marina Milyavskaya, a professor of psychology at Carleton University in Ottawa, Canada and her colleagues from McGill University in Montreal, conducted a study examining the social-psychological basis of FOMO in Gen Z.[88]

Milyavskaya and her colleagues started their first study by having a group of first-year university students with smartphones complete a diary for one week. Throughout each day, the students received five alerts including a link to a survey asking about their well-being and satisfaction with their present experiences. This was followed by an online questionnaire on their overall well-being and satisfaction at the end of the study.

The results of the study showed people whose behaviors felt more like personal obligations, including *studying* or *working*, were more likely to report greater FOMO. This was also associated with negative outcomes such as stress, sleep issues, fatigue, and other psychosomatic symptoms.

In a follow-up study, the researchers placed the participants in an imaginary scenario where they had found out about a planned social activity for the evening while also learning about the possible option of an alternate activity. The alternative activities could be social or not, and the participant

88 Marina Milyavskaya et al. "Fear of Missing Out: Prevalence, Dynamics, and Consequences of Experiencing FOMO," *Motivation and Emotion*, 42 (March 17, 2018): 725-737, accessed June 4, 2020.

was asked to imagine being "reminded" of the alternate social activity. For example a party, either through a friend or social media notification.

In the imagined scenario, the large majority of the participants reported having FOMO and feeling a negative emotion because they couldn't do both activities at once. The results also showed the participants possessed FOMO even when their planned activity was enjoyable.

I had the opportunity to speak with Dana-Maxx, the founder of The Be Happy Project, which is a positivity platform featuring inspiring content related to inner happiness, self-love, and personal growth. She said, "When we look at how much we need to do throughout our days, it's easy for our minds to start racing and for stuff to pile up. When you get overwhelmed, your body tenses up and you then tie that emotion to the activities you want to get done during your day, which prolongs their completion. These are the times where it's most important to have an outlet in your day."

So what can we do about our busy lives and the feeling of FOMO which seems to arise so often? How does our happiness fit into the busyness equation? Well Ed Diener, who is currently a professor of psychology at the University of Utah and the University of Virginia, and Martin Seligman, who is a professor of psychology at the University of Pennsylvania, were interested in that very topic. They published a famous psychological study titled "Very Happy People" in 2002.[89]

---

89   Ed Diener and M.E.P. Seligman "Very Happy People," *eddiener.com*, 2002, accessed June 5, 2020.

In the study, Diener and Seligman screened 222 undergraduates for high happiness through multiple confirming assessment filters. Diener and Seligman took the undergraduates in the study who consistently scored in the top 10 percent of the happiness surveys and compared them to those who scored in the average or below-average categories for overall happiness.

They found the biggest difference between the top 10 percent and the rest of the undergraduates in the study was they were more social and spent more time around other people. Diener and Seligman concluded spending time with other people and being social on a consistent basis was a *necessary* component in attaining a high level of happiness.

Behavioral scientists Nicholas Epley and Juliana Schroeder conducted a 2014 study on Chicago area train commuters to see how their happiness would be affected if they talked to strangers during their commute. Epley and Schroeder asked one group of participants to talk to the stranger who sat down next to them on the train that morning, and they told a separate group to follow standard commuter norms and keep to themselves.[90]

Before they boarded the train, the participants in the group asked to talk to the stranger who sat next to them estimated only about 40 percent of their fellow train passengers would be willing to talk to them. However, Epley and Schroeder found 100 percent of the participants in the experiment who

---

90   Michael Norton and Elizabeth W. Dunn, "Conversation Class," *Princeton Conversation Group* (blog), May 15, 2014, accessed June 6, 2020.

attempted to speak with a stranger got a response. Epley and Schroeder surveyed the commuters at the end and found the commuters who spoke with strangers reported having a more positive experience than those who did not speak with anyone.

Upon learning this, in the fall of my senior year of college I decided to incorporate one new thing into my morning goal visualization every day: have a positive interaction with one new person today. No matter how busy I felt or how much I'm moving around, I was always trying to find new ways to accomplish this goal.

I started by smiling and saying "hi" to a stranger on the street each day. I challenged myself to have a conversation with a stranger during an elevator ride up to my floor at work and telling the cashier to have a great day at the checkout counter.

This daily goal for myself wasn't contingent on the stranger's response. It was about me reaching out and socializing with someone new. For the first few weeks I implemented this daily goal, I got a lot of smiles and "hi's" in return, but there was one specific day I can't forget.

I had gotten on the elevator in the lobby of my office building after grabbing lunch and as the doors started to close after I hit the button for my floor, a lady came running across the marble floor yelling "Hold it, please!"

I held the door for her, and she got into the elevator next to me. She stood off to the opposite wall and stared straight forward at the metal doors as most people do when they get into an elevator with a stranger. She had pushed the button for the tenth floor, so there was time for a conversation.

I turned to her and said, "Hey, so how's the day going so far?"

She looked back at me kind of surprised and said, "Um... pretty good how are you?"

I asked her what she did for work, and by the time she finished explaining, the elevator dinged and the doors opened to the tenth floor.

As she walked out, I said, "It was nice meeting you. Have a great day."

She turned back and said, "You too. And thank you for talking to me. Most kids your age would just be on their phones, but that made my day."

This kind of floored me. I didn't really feel like I had done very much, but the lady said I "made her day." It was so simple to say those few words during the elevator ride, yet she said most kids my age didn't. That experience drove home the importance of socializing with others and how it correlates with happiness.

University of Georgia relief pitcher Will Proctor summed this up well. He said, "When you look at the big picture, the adage 'time really flies' holds true when you look at the past. But when we think about the future, it seems like it will be an eternity. It all comes down to the fact that our time each day is an opportunity. If spending an hour with friends during my day causes me to have one less hour of sleep, then I'm willing to put in that time because it's important."

Amidst the expectations to be busy, we have the opportunity each day to interact with others and make someone's day better. We have the ability to talk to a complete stranger and make a positive impact on their day. In our busy days, socializing with others is a choice we have every day which can bring us happiness and change the stigma of the "being busy" status symbol for working-age people in America.

CHAPTER 19

STEP ON THE CRACKS, APPRECIATE THE WORLD, AND KEEP THE OIL ON THE SPOON

———

"A mental prison is fashioned from our own hand. The bars are wrought with metal from our fears and anxieties. But, for as trapped as we may feel, we just need to look in our back pocket for the key to our cell, turn the lock, and step outside. When you do leave your cell, step on the cracks."

—BRANDON POSIVAK

Well, we made it. This is the conclusion of our journey together through these pages, but the beginning of our lives in the real world. Early on in our journey, we left the binoculars behind and picked up the glasses to fully see our happiness. We delved deep into concepts embodying the struggles of Gen Z in today's world and uncovered what it means to possess our individual happiness fingerprint.

Now is a time for action. Past statistics, personal anecdotes, and wanting to live happier lives, it is now up to us as a generation to write our own story. It is up to us to persist through challenges and find our own happiness and success in life. This may seem like a daunting task, but there is a starting point: *step on the cracks.*

As discussed early on in the journey, this is my reminder to reset when I feel mentally locked up or frustrated and to keep my mind free and clear throughout my day as I pursue my path. What's yours? If there isn't one coming to mind, make a list and narrow it down to a couple you like. Those phrases will be unique to you and will help keep you focused on your ultimate goal of finding happiness when doubt or exhaustion sets in.

What we are trying to accomplish as a generation is incredibly difficult. We want to make a difference and leave our mark. We want to thrive in our careers, be financially secure, and help others as we embark on our personal and professional journeys. By using our positivity and optimism tools, and through our desires and goals, we want to be happy and live a joyous life.

As we inherit this world, I want to share one final story. The story comes from Paulo Coelho's *The Alchemist* and is titled "The Secret of Happiness." I have purposely left this story for the end of our journey together.[91]

---

91   Paulo Coelho, *The Alchemist,* 25th ed. (New York: Harper Collins, 2014).

In the story, a young man desires more than anything to learn the secret of happiness. He travels a great distance to a scenic castle atop of a mountain where the wisest man in the world lived.

The young man expected a sage, simple sanctuary, but instead saw people conversing, an orchestra playing music, and a table covered with platters of the most delicious food.

The young man waited several hours for the wise man to finish conversing with his guests, and when he had the wise man's attention he asked the question which had burned in his mind for so long: "What is the secret to happiness?."

The wise man answered by handing the young man a spoon with two drops of oil on it and giving him two directions: look around the castle and appreciate its beauty, and do not let the oil spill off the spoon.

The young man left the castle and walked around the surrounding areas, keeping his eyes fixed on the spoon as if his life depended on it. He returned to the wise man and showed him the intact oil on the spoon.

The wise man looks and says, "Well? Did you see the Persian embroideries that are hanging in my dining hall? Did you see the garden that it took the master gardener ten years to create? Did you notice the beautiful parchments in the library?"

The young man admitted he hadn't seen any of it because he was solely concerned about not spilling the oil.

The wise man says, "Then go back and observe the marvels of my world. You cannot trust a man if you know nothing about that man and his surroundings."

So the young man once again went outside and this time really tried to take in the beauty of the surrounding areas. He returned to the wise man and described all of the beauty in detail.

The wise man listens then asks, "But where are the drops of oil I entrusted to you?"

The young man looked down at his spoon and realized the oil was gone.

The wise man says, "Well, there is only one piece of advice I can give you. The secret of happiness is to see all the marvels of the world, and never to forget the drops of oil on the spoon."

This story shows us everything in our lives requires a balance. We have the right to enjoy the beauty and pleasures of the world, but we have to fulfill our duties as well. If we lean too far in one direction or the other, our life balance is lost along with our happiness.

Happiness is hard and takes work and constant upkeep to maintain. There is no destination we can get to where we are happy 100 percent of the time. People, money, technology, and jobs will all come in and out of our lives, but our happiness fingerprint is something we can always improve.

It isn't possible to be happy all the time, but it is possible to gradually become happier for longer and more frequent periods of time. Harvard University Psychology Professor Daniel Gilbert says, "People think happiness is a house they can build and live there their entire lives." Gilbert goes on to say happiness is like a vacation destination. We can visit this spot more often and stay longer if we do the right things. However, we cannot stay forever.

On this journey, we put down the binoculars and picked up the glasses to see happiness in a more holistic, all-encompassing way. Through this perspective, we better visualize both how we can be happy and how we can use our new perspective to positively affect others. The bad times make the good times better, and it is in the bad times we are truly able to appreciate the goodness in our lives. My dad always told me when I would get down on myself, "No matter what happens, your toes are still tapping."

Comparing ourselves to others on social media, leaning too heavily on our cell phones and video games, and fearing unpredictability of our careers and futures are all impediments to our happiness as a generation. They are mental blocks to our positive perspective, and when we only see the negatives and our misfortunes in life, that's what will become our reality. If we see the silver linings and recognize our ability to bring positivity to our lives each day, positivity will become our reality.

We are not defined by the bad times in our lives, and they can only steal our happiness if we let them. We are in control of our happiness, and each day we have the ability to exercise this control. That's a special gift, and it is never too late to realize we possess it.

Life is unfair and it won't do us any favors. For my fellow members of Gen Z, we are starting our lives in this world, and to make the greatest impact we can we need to put ourselves in the best position to be happy. Be comfortable in your own skin and take pride in your happiness fingerprint. Understand you truly have a superpower. You have the ability to bring positivity to the lives of others. I have seen first-hand how powerful this can be, and it is one of the greatest gifts a human being can possibly give to another. Don't pursue happiness. Realize happiness is inside of you. Don't just try to be positive; spread it to others. Don't just be optimistic about the future but will your optimistic thoughts into reality.

I'm grateful to have embarked on this journey to reinventing happiness, positivity, and optimism with you. If you can take away only one thing from these words, take away the idea happiness is achievable and you have the gift of giving it to others as well. Use what you have learned in this book to better yourself and those around you each and every day. When the world remembers Gen Z, they will remember us not for our lucrative careers or how much money we pumped into the economy. They will remember us for how we created happiness, positivity, and optimism in the world.

The future is yet to be written, so grab a pen and let's write one hell of a story for ourselves. We rise together, we fall together, and we support one another. The unpredictability ahead of us should be an exciting motivator because there is a world of opportunity for us, and we are ready for it. In our first chapter together, I shared Roy T. Bennett's quote which said, "Be the reason someone smiles today. Be the reason someone feels loved and believes in the goodness of people." For my fellow members of Gen Z, it's our time now. Let's be that reason.

ACKNOWLEDGMENTS

———

My sincerest gratitude to Professor Eric Koester and Brian Bies for believing in this book from the very beginning and for pushing me every step along the way in this incredible journey.

I also want to thank my editors—Katie Sigler, Jessica Drake-Thomas, Anne Belott—for helping turn the vision for this book into an amazing reality to be shared with the world.

Thank you to the rest of the team at New Degree Press—Amanda Knox, Gjorgji Pevkovski, Matuesz Cichosz, Haley Newlin, Lyn Solares, Jamie T.—for their patience and guidance throughout the writing process and for answering my many questions.

Thank you to my incredible family—Todd Posivak, Linda Posivak, Nico Posivak, Tom Posivak, Marilyn Joffee, Haydee Navarette, Michael Arkof, Dann Fink, Michelle Del Guercio, Norma Freeman, the Connor family, the McBride family, the Deary family, the Topar family—for their never-ending support and encouragement while creating this book and throughout my entire life.

Thank you to my all my former teammates—Henry Welsh, Alex Goodman, Daniel Caruso, Hunter Tiedemann, Riley Livingston, Alonzo Billips, Will Proctor, Quinn Brodey, Dustin Shirley, Richie O'Reilly, Jackson Kritsch, Blake Beers, Ryan Demarest, Jake Suddleson, Joe Morin, Tom Fuller, McCabe Slye, Chuck Nelson, Kyle Mashy, Andres Paco Kim, Andrew Shults, Morgan West, Race Gardner, Zach Liebenson, Collin Valdivia, RC Orozco, Nathan Garko, Drew Jansen, John Marti, Brett Kreyer, Mark Glover, Luke Robinson, Coleman Strohm, Alex Woinski, Trevor Houck, Gabe Levine, Dan Leckie, Conor Russell, Spencer Rouse, Kyle Johnson, Zeke Berg, David Giusti—for your support both on and off the field. Getting to play alongside you will always be one of the highlights of my life.

Thank you to the members of *Full Lope So Steez*—Drew Slipe, Will Minck, Armen Deirmenjian, Chris Novia, Finn Veje, Tommy Vossler, Tommy Von Der Ahe, Brandon Bueno—for always having my back through thick and thin.

Thank you to my high school friends: Matthew Friedman, Zach Profozich, Henry Hawley, Will Mamer, Osa Adler, Caitlin Keefe, Michaela Keefe, Sean Smith, Emily Newberry, Rob Mullahey, Kirsten Ahn, Matt Bland, Adrian Sibal, Andrue Delgado, Terence Roquemore, Claire Meylan, Trejon Shelton, J.P. Barrett, Allison Gist, James Marquez, Gabriel Schneider, Lorenzo Poto, Penny Walsh, Akinty Carter, Jorge Ulloa, Luc Daniels, Rasheed Clarke, Rachel Yanofsky, Connor Ladwig, Maximiliano Neblina, Calvin Yi, Joe Walker, Noah Utley,

Tommy Atlee, Andy Begazo,Thomas Knight, Peter Rizko, Madison McKesson, Justin Wang, Nahom Seifu, Ryan Deutsch, Jack Rothman, and Leyton McNamara.

Thank you to my college friends—Jillian Turkmany, Katherine Addy, Regan Kinney, Sonia Musso, Christian Luhnow, Dylan Murphy, Natasha Miner, Alex DeSantis, Myles Harris, Dylan Royalty, Parker Gaglione, Tim Barry, Adam Finklestein, Brad Seeber, Meredith Block, Bella Alampi, Ryan Monteyne, Cal Reichwein, Katherine Stevens, Zane Crandall, Stacy Gordon, Tali Dressler, Allie Abacherli, Sophia Carr, Alex Mezey, Max Kushner, Katrina Ruggiero, Cooper Ochsenhirt, Jeff Sikorsky, Maggie Sahnnon, Sophia Gardinier, Quinn Lacy, Amy Hewlett, Frank Clarke, Charlie Hoyt, Josh Hubbard, Peter Bokma, Philip Arnett, Pascual Ventura—for always checking in and for the nudges of support over the past year.

Thank you to the legendary *Dinger:* Andrew Harvell, Nathaniel Haas, Mike Mottweiler, Ellen Corn, Mike Smigielski, Mike Rizzo, Allen Butler, and Adam Gold.

Thank you to the gentlemen of *Yoi Minoy:* Trey Fearn, Connor Scanlan, Michael Vogeler, Kenny Resch, Greyson Bromber, Blake Randall, and Drew Erb.

Thank you to my law school group, *Capitol Offense*—Curtis Crawford, Patrick Ryan, Michael Elterman, Ben Pollock, Jake Kammersgard, Bobby Stern, Tyler Lisea, Sean Fox, Daniel Foster, Aaron Bausch, Brittany Farias, Josphine Klein, Gigi Grasska, Mikaela Clinton, Emily Olsen, Lilah Cook, Megan Hamilton, Emma Erikson-Kerry, John McPherson,

Abby Falk, Tess Schiesl, Olivia Davis, Amelia Tidwell, Kelly Mahoney, Tatum Lowe, Thurgood Wynn, Ricky Wolsford, Caroline Clouse—for all those long nights spent studying and for reminding me there's always fun to be had if you take the time to look for it.

You should never forget your roots, and my Cheviot Hills roots have made me who I am today. For this reason, I would like to thank Owen Rothman, Tyler Yeh, Eli Salzman, Isaiah Volk, Gabe Okmin, Jonathan Phelps, Sean O'Malley, Tom Batan, Wakelin McNeel, Adam Benezra, Ben Krieger, Jonah Dylan, Jake Taitelman, and Henry Ward for sharing your excitement of the book with others.

Thank you to my mentors, teachers, coaches, and coworkers who, through thick and thin, taught me so many life lessons and guided me on the right path at each stage of life: TJ Runnels, Tye Gonser, Jordan Matthews, Bryan Bitzer, Joel Sherwin, Kylee MacArthur, Yaffa Shamy, Ryan Adcock, Shahrokh Shiek, Jon Zimmerman, Bob Rudd, Raymond Hall, Vince Fraga, Tina Maokhampio, Stella D'Arceaux, Sylvie Griffith, Grant Chen, Rich Keller, Joseph Lalonde, Susan Salzman, Tom Peck, Stewart E. Hayes, Eric Romin, Mike Barnhill, Sean Buller, John Amer, Matt Schaeffer, Tanner Biagini, Tony Testa, Kyle Knoll, Luke Mohatt, Michael Olin, Michael Summers, Patricia Salvaty, Robert Rosenstock, Brett Henry, Noriko Nakada, Kyle Morrison, Nathan Peralta, Chung Wu, and Diana Greenstein.

I would also like to thank all my fellow authors who helped so much along this journey and who continuously pushed me day in and day out: Haley Newlin, Amy Dong, Nicole

Spindler, Massimo Marchiano, Josh Lasky, Lauren Stike-
leather, Andrew Feinstein, Juan David Campolargo, Elizabeth Ivanecky, Emily VanderBent, John Saunders, Adam
Arafat, Anjana Sreedhar, Jessica McCarter, Carole Sprunk,
Nicholas D'Souza, Mary Yuan, and Esther Kim.

A special thank you to Sophie Pollack for her bravery, courage, and passion for helping others. Your story has and will
continue to touch so many, and I'm honored to have you as
part of this book.

Thank you as well to Dana-Maxx Pomerantz, Jennifer Chaeng,
Kaito Irizarry, Victoria Anderson, Tristan Crowder, Lindsey
Griffith, Jayne Cooper, Peter Slyman, Anne Butler, Dianne
King, Cindy Gold, Stefan Pollack, Tinker Lindsey, Cameron
Keyes, Tricia Dierks, Lauren Barry, Jana Shemano, the Sehi-
doglou family, Elliot Brooks, Jesse Shapiro, Scott Morris, the
Kirschbaum family, Portia Profozich, Art and Sarita Cohen,
Kathy O'Malley, Laura Mamer, Julee Madkins, Laurie Tie-
demann, Holly Culhane, Pam Reynolds, Dana Ching, Matt
Donovan, Louise Brown, Mara Benitez, Tamara Bland, Mark
Weinstein, Karen Crawford, Kristine Berglund, and Karen
Hartley.

APPENDIX

———

AUTHOR'S NOTE:

Bennett, Roy T. *The Light in the Heart: Inspirational Thoughts for Living Your Best Life.* Roy T. Bennett, 2016.

Dimock, Michael. "Defining Generations: Where Millennials End and Generation Z Begins." *Pew Research Center,* January 17, 2019. https://www.pewresearch.org/fact-tank/2019/01/17/where-millennials-end-and-generation-z-begins/.

Gilbert, Daniel. *Stumbling on Happiness.* New York: Random House, 2007.

Mackey, Harvey, and Kenneth H. Blanchard. *Swim with the Sharks: Without Being Eaten Alive.* London: Sphere, 2013.

Waitley, Denis. *Seeds of Greatness: Ten Best-kept Secrets of Total Success.* Ringwood, Victoria: Brolga Publications, 1994.

CHAPTER 1: YOU MAY NOT SEE WHERE IT LEADS, BUT TAKE THE LEAP WITH ME

Fleming, Victor, dir. *The Wizard of Oz*. 1939; Beverly Hills, CA: Metro-Goldwyn-Mayer.

CHAPTER 2: APPEARANCES ARE DECEIVING, BUT ENERGY VAMPIRES HAVE NO SEAT ON THE ENERGY BUS

"Annual Gen Z Research Studies – Trends, Stats, Attitudes & More." The Center for Generational Kinetics. Last modified July 24, 2020. Accessed April 11, 2020. https://genhq.com/annual-gen-z-research-study/.

"The Common Sense Census: Plugged-In Parents of Tweens and Teens, 2016: Common Sense Media." *Common Sense Media: Ratings, Reviews, and Advice*. Last modified December 06, 2016. Accessed August 31, 2020. https://www.commonsensemedia.org/research/the-common-sense-census-plugged-in-parents-of-tweens-and-teens-2016.

Gordon, Jon. *The Energy Bus: 10 Rules to Fuel Your Life, Work, and Team with Positive Energy*. Chichester, West Sussex: Wiley, 2015.

McAteer, Oliver. "Gen Z Is Quitting Social Media in Droves Because It Makes Them Unhappy, Study Finds." *Brand Knew Magazine*. Last modified March 14, 2018. Accessed Mar. 2, 2020. https://www.brandknewmag.com/gen-z-is-quitting-social-media-in-droves-because-it-makes-them-unhappy-study-finds/.

CHAPTER 3: SYNTHETIC HAPPINESS IS TEMPORARY, BUT JOY REMAINS AN INTERNAL CONSTANT

Dispenza, Joe. *Breaking the Habit of Being Yourself: How to Lose Your Mind and Create a New One.* Carlsbad, CA: Hay House, 2016.

Eston, Echo. "Theology of Joy: Robert Emmons with Matt Croasmun." *YouTube.* Last modified September 25, 2014. Accessed May 1, 2020. https://www.youtube.com/watch?v=CxDOVQK-Kp5c.

Gilbert, Daniel. *Stumbling on Happiness.* New York: Random House, 2007.

Gilbert, Daniel. "Why We Make Bad Decisions." *TED.* Last modified July 2005. Accessed April 29, 2020. https://www.ted.com/talks/dan_gilbert_why_we_make_bad_decisions.

Gilbert, Daniel. "The Surprising Science of Happiness." *TED.* Last modified February 2004. Accessed May 2, 2020. https://www.ted.com/talks/dan_gilbert_the_surprising_science_of_happiness.

CHAPTER 4: PETER PAN WANTS TO STAY A KID, BUT HE TAUGHT ME HOW TO GROW UP

Albo, Mike. "The True Story Behind Peter Pan Is Kind of Crazy." *Refinery 29.* Vice Media Group, December 3, 2014. Accessed April 6, 2020. https://www.refinery29.com/en-us/2014/12/78880/peter-pan-jm-barrie-true-story.

Coraci, Frank, dir. *Click*. 2006; Los Angeles, CA: Columbia Productions.

Steers, Burr, dir. *17 Again*. 2009; Santa Monica, CA: New Line Cinema.

Waters, Mark, dir. *Freaky Friday*. 2003; Santa Monica, CA; Walt Disney Productions.

CHAPTER 5: QUITTING IS EASY, BUT DELAYED GRATIFICATION IS FOR THOSE WHO PERSIST

Fitz-Gibbon, Jorge. "'Grit' More Important to Success than Brains and Brawn, West Point Study Finds." *New York Post*. November 04, 2019. Accessed March 6, 2020. https://nypost.com/2019/11/04/grit-more-important-to-success-than-brains-and-brawn-west-point-study-finds/.

Hill, Napoleon. *Think and Grow Rich*. London: Penguin Group, 2005.

Kaba, Rhodel. "Here's What You Need to Know About Generation Z." *The Digital Strategy & Marketing Blog* (blog). *Rhodel.com*, June 26, 2014. Accessed March 7, 2020. https://rhodel.com/2014/06/heres-what-you-need-to-know-about-generation-z/.

"The Stanford Marshmallow Experiment: How Self-Control Affects Your Success in Life." *Effectiviology*. Accessed March 8, 2020. https://effectiviology.com/stanford-marshmallow-experiment-self-control-willpower/.

CHAPTER 6: SHE MAY NOT HAVE HER SIGHT, BUT SHE HELPED ME SEE

"APA Stress in America™ Survey: Generation Z Stressed About Issues in the News but Least Likely to Vote." American Psychological Association, October 30, 2018. Accessed March 19, 2020. https://www.apa.org/news/press/releases/2018/10/generation-z-stressed.

"Bullying is Gen Z's #1 Concern According to New BSA Survey." *Scouting Newsroom* (blog). Boy Scouts of America, September 17, 2019. Accessed March 26, 2020. https://www.scoutingnewsroom.org/press-releases/bullying-is-gen-zs-1-concern-according-to-new-bsa-survey/.

Loney, Sydney. "Blind and Bullied: Teenage Activist Molly Burke Shares Her Inspirational Story." *Chatelaine*, January 18, 2017. Accessed Mar. 9, 2020. https://www.chatelaine.com/living/real-life-stories/blind-and-bullied-teenage-activist-molly-burke-shares-her-inspirational-story/.

Mastroianni, Brian. "How Generation Z Is Changing the Tech World." *CBS News*, March 10, 2016. Accessed April 21, 2020. https://www.cbsnews.com/news/social-media-fuels-a-change-in-generations-with-the-rise-of-gen-z/.

CHAPTER 7: THE DAY MAY BE LONG, BUT I START BY MAKING MY BED

"Adm. McRaven Urges Graduates to Find Courage to Change the World." *UT News*. The University of Texas at Austin, May 16, 2014. Accessed Mar. 21, 2020. https://news.utexas.edu/

2014/05/16/mcraven-urges-graduates-to-find-courage-to-change-the-world/.

"APA Stress in America™ Survey: Generation Z Stressed About Issues in the News but Least Likely to Vote." American Psychological Association, October 30, 2018. Accessed March 19, 2020. https://www.apa.org/news/press/releases/2018/10/generation-z-stressed.

Chatterjee, Rangan. *Stress Solution: The 4 Steps to Reset Your Body, Mind, Relationships and Purpose.* London: Penguin Books, 2019.

Robbins, Mel. "The 5 Second Rule." *Mel Robbins* (blog), December 13, 2018. Accessed May 7, 2020. https://melrobbins.com/the-5-second-rule/.

"Stress on Disease." Carnegie Mellon University. Accessed Mar. 14, 2020. https://www.cmu.edu/homepage/health/2012/spring/stress-on-disease.shtml#:~:text=A%20research%20team%20led%20by%20Carnegie%20Mellon%20University%27s,can%20promote%20the%20development%20and%20progression%20of%20disease.

"Stress Symptoms: Effects on Your Body and Behavior." Mayo Clinic, April 04, 2019. Accessed May 22, 2020. https://www.mayoclinic.org/healthy-lifestyle/stress-management/in-depth/stress-symptoms/art-20050987.

Williams, Robert. "Gen Z Prefers Entertainment, Social Media in Early Dayparts." *Mobile Marketer*, November 22, 2019. Accessed May 16, 2020. https://www.mobilemarketer.com/

news/gen-z-prefers-entertainment-social-media-in-early-day-parts/567877/.

CHAPTER 8: WORK ISN'T ALWAYS FUN, BUT I'M A GOLDEN RETRIEVER

European Society of Cardiology. "Global Study Sheds Light on Role of Exercise, Cars and Televisions on the Risk of Heart Attacks." *ScienceDaily*, January 11, 2012. Accessed Apr. 19, 2020. https://www.sciencedaily.com/releases/2012/01/120111090611.htm.

Gilbert, Daniel. *Stumbling on Happiness*. New York: Random House, 2007.

Vaynerchuck, Gary. "Business Tips: Why You Hate 64.28% of Your Life/ A Gary Vaynerchuck Original." *Biz Channel Review Guide,* December 19, 2019. Accessed Mar. 29, 2020. https://www.superinspirednow.com/gary-vaynerchuk/why-do-you-hate-64-28-of-your-life-a-gary-vaynerchuk-original/.

CHAPTER 9: MY LIFE IS A ROLLER COASTER, BUT UNPREDICTABILITY CREATES OPPORTUNITY

"Gen Z Feels They Work the Hardest, Says New Workforce Institute at Kronos Research." *HR Dive*, June 11, 2019. Accessed May 8, 2020. https://www.hrdive.com/press-release/20190611-gen-z-feels-they-work-the-hardest-says-new-workforce-institute-at-kronos-r/.

Markman, Art. "Unpredictability Is in Our Nature." *Psychology Today*, November 17, 2008. Accessed May 10, 2020. https://www.

psychologytoday.com/us/blog/ulterior-motives/200811/unpredictability-is-in-our-nature.

"Reduce the Options You Give Your Customers and Get 30% More Conversions," *Usability Testing* (blog). Conversion Hub. Accessed May 16, 2020. https://usabilitytesting.sg/blog/web-usability/options-give-customers-30-more-conversions/.

CHAPTER 10: BEFORE IT WAS SURVIVING, BUT TODAY IT'S THRIVING

"90 Percent of Gen Z Tired of How Negative and Divided Our Country Is Around Important Issues, According to Research by Porter Novelli/Cone." *Yahoo! Finance.* Yahoo, October 23, 2019. Accessed April 15, 2020. https://finance.yahoo.com/news/90-percent-gen-z-tired-141500365.html?guccounter=1&guce_referrer=aHR0cHM6Ly93d3cuYmluZy5jb20v&guce_referrer_sig=AQAAAL7duC7CUuoSo4FRo4qLd-_VQVFq858hFi5R-fz-28jCsr_4CgQtq_AXIqg4uYnXgMKcy9SzZWTH-YaByHFEd-WQWACCWJoBR8itR5xHHKXaooy3OPxcxyDJutT8RDGhF-Pbnx3_90H9Vheh9eWw2WZrivW-TVtE_ZMMwh6w3sw1zJ2.

Akbari, Anna. "Surviving vs. Thriving." *Psychology Today.* Sussex Publishers, December 16, 2019. Accessed May 14, 2020. https://www.psychologytoday.com/us/blog/startup-your-life/201912/surviving-vs-thriving.

Francis, David R. "Why Do Death Rates Decline?" The National Bureau of Economic Research. Accessed April 24, 2020. https://www.nber.org/digest/mar02/w8556.html.

"Gen Z: Preparing to Face the Future." UniDAYS. https://corporate. myunidays.com/en-us/research-and-insights.

CHAPTER 11: NEGATIVITY IS POWERFUL, BUT I FEED MY GOOD WOLF MORE

"APA Stress in America Survey: Generation Z Stressed About Issues in the News but Least Likely to Vote." American Psychological Association, October 30, 2018. Accessed March 30, 2020. https://www.apa.org/news/press/releases/2018/10/generation-z-stressed.

Buchholz, Katharina. "Infographic: Number of School Shootings Increased Every Decade." *Statista Infographics*, November 15, 2019. Accessed May 12, 2020. https://www.statista.com/chart/19982/number-of-us-k-12-school-shootings-per-decade/.

CHAPTER 12: MONEY IS IMPORTANT, BUT FOR GEN Z, CASH IS KING

Amadeo, Kimberly. "How Does the 2020 Stock Market Compare with Others?" *The Balance*, April 27, 2020. Accessed May 19, 2020. https://www.thebalance.com/fundamentals-of-the-2020-market-crash-4799950.

"APA Stress in America™ Survey: Generation Z Stressed About Issues in the News but Least Likely to Vote." American Psychological Association, October 30, 2018. Accessed March 31, 2020. https://www.apa.org/news/press/releases/2018/10/generation-z-stressed.

Martinez, Gina. "Everything You Know About the Fate of Lottery Winners Is Probably Wrong." *Time*. Time, October 18, 2018. Accessed May 23, 2020. https://time.com/5427275/lottery-winning-happiness-debunked/.

McConaughey, Matthew. "Matthew McConaughey to Grads: Always Play Like an Underdog." *Time*. Time, May 17, 2015. Accessed May 20, 2020. https://time.com/collection-post/3881954/matthew-mcconaughey-graduation-speech-university-of-houston/.

Porter, Edward, and David Yaffe-Bellany. "Facing Adulthood with an Economic Disaster's Lasting Scars." *The New York Times*. The New York Times, May 19, 2020. Accessed May 20, 2020. https://www.nytimes.com/2020/05/19/business/economy/coronavirus-young-old.html.

CHAPTER 13: TECHNOLOGY ALLOWS US TO FACETIME, BUT GEN Z WANTS FACE TIME

Boucher, Jared. "Top 10 Gen Z Statistics from 2018." The Center for Generational Kinetics. Accessed May 23, 2020. https://genhq.com/top-10-ways-gen-z-is-shaping-the-future/.

Hilliard, Jena. "New Study Reveals Gen Z as the Loneliest Generation in America." Addiction Center, last modified June 18, 2020. Accessed May 20, 2020. https://www.addictioncenter.com/news/2019/08/gen-z-loneliest-generation/.

Jenkins, Ryan. "Who Is Generation Z? This Timeline Reveals It All." *Inc.com*, September 25, 2017. Accessed May 22, 2020. https://

blog.ryan-jenkins.com/who-is-generation-z-this-timeline-reveals-it-all.

Krawczyk, Konrad. "87 Percent of U.S. Adults Use the 'net, and Other Fun Pew Research Stats." *Digital Trends*, February 27, 2014. Accessed May 21, 2020. https://www.digitaltrends.com/computing/87-percent-american-adults-use-net-pew-research-center-stats/.

LivePerson, Inc. "Gen Z and Millennials Now More Likely to Communicate with Each Other Digitally than in Person." *PR Newswire*, October 17, 2017. Accessed May 25, 2020. https://www.prnewswire.com/news-releases/gen-z-and-millennials-now-more-likely-to-communicate-with-each-other-digitally-than-in-person-300537770.html.

"Mobile Kids: The Parent, the Child and the Smartphone." *Nielsen.com*. The Nielsen Company, February 28, 2017. Accessed May 22, 2020. https://www.nielsen.com/us/en/insights/article/2017/mobile-kids-the-parent-the-child-and-the-smartphone/.

"Reader Opinion: CommScope Research on Gen Z Reveals an Always-On Mindset." *Inside Towers*, October 18, 2017. Accessed May 19, 2020. https://insidetowers.com/commscope-research-gen-z-reveals-always-mindset/.

Stars Insider. "How Much Do You Know about Generation Z?" *MSN*. Microsoft News. Accessed May 21, 2020. https://www.msn.com/en-gb/money/technology/how-much-do-you-know-about-gen-z/ss-BBZT9j4.

CHAPTER 14: THE FOCUS IS ON MAKING A LIVING, BUT WE WANT TO MAKE A LIFE FOR OURSELVES

Andraos, Rania Merchak. "Looking at the Glass Half Full in the Translation Business." *TransPremium.com* (blog). TransPremium Translation, August 25, 2015. Accessed June 1, 2020. http://transpremium.com/looking-at-the-glass-half-full-in-the-translation-business/.

Entrepreneur Staff. "41 Percent of Gen Z-ers Plan to Become Entrepreneurs (Infographic)." *Entrepreneur.* Entrepreneur Media, January 15, 2019. Accessed June 2, 2020. https://www.entrepreneur.com/article/326354.

"Gen Z and Morality: What Teens Believe (So Far)." Barna Group, October 9, 2018. Accessed May 30, 2020.

Perna, Mark C. "Gen Z Wants to Change the World— At Your Company." *Forbes.* Forbes Media, December 19, 2019. Accessed June 1, 2020. https://www.forbes.com/sites/markcperna/2019/12/10/gen-z-wants-to-change-the-world-at-your-company/#565034043c56.

Team CGK. "Generation Z Wants a Job." The Center for Generational Kinetics. Accessed May 29, 2020. https://genhq.com/generation-z-wants-job/.

CHAPTER 15: THE "WHAT" AND THE "HOW" SET OUR PATH, BUT THE "WHY" MAKES IT UNIQUE

Gregoire, Carolyn. "How Being an Oldest, Middle or Youngest Child Shapes Your Personality." *HuffPost Science*, last modified May 15, 2015. Accessed May 27, 2020. https://www.

huffpost.com/entry/birth-order-personality_n_7206252?gu-ccounter=1&guce_referrer=aHR0cHM6Ly93d3cuYmluZy55jb2ov&guce_referrer_sig=AQAAALo3ErNjfdzQfyno3hiCs-5DrUZM1e9B8jQUn_DYRhCfEEfRggoUdxQk13Mx-rNr-lYkhYKmox_xpWSvZiMBrlo5XYeN64L0NJT98zP4mUGjAfSMaBbbsbbPcBmJC0pRVNRZv9OCYlLmPp27WAsk_Lw-d1REhlNkinUlj6FTiaJnsf.

Sinek, Simon. "How Great Leaders Inspire Action." *TEDx Puget Sound*, last modified September 2009. Accessed May 29, 2020. https://www.ted.com/talks/simon_sinek_how_great_leaders_inspire_action.

Smith, Michael. "Studies Show That Children Just Want to Be Famous." *Guardian Liberty Voice*. Guardian Liberty Voice, August 3, 2013. Accessed June 3, 2020. https://guardianlv.com/2013/08/studies-show-that-children-just-want-to-be-famous/.

University of California Los Angeles. "Popular TV Shows Teach Children Fame Is Most Important Value, Psychologists Report; Being Kind to Others Fell Dramatically in Importance over 10 Years." *ScienceDaily*. ScienceDaily, July 22, 2011. Accessed June 3, 2020. https://www.sciencedaily.com/releases/2011/07/110712094237.htm.

CHAPTER 16: RIDE THAT WAVE, BUT FIND THAT REFERENCE POINT

Gilovich Medvec, T., V.H. Madey, and S.F. Gilovich. "When Less Is More: Counterfactual Thinking and Satisfaction among Olympic Medalists." *Journal of Personality and Social Psychology* 69, no. 4 (October 1995): 603–10. doi: 10.1037//0022-3514.69.4.603.

Gutting, Casey, Yahoo! Sports. February 22, 2018. Accessed April 19, 2020. Hhttps://sports.yahoo.com/usa-wins-hockey-gold-canadian-player-promptly-removes-silver-medal-presentation-081201056.html.

Shetty, Jay. "Redefining Happiness: Street Philosophy with Jay Shetty." *HuffPost*, September 15, 2016. Accessed March 16, 2020. https://www.youtube.com/watch?v=_R6R62qUgIs .

CHAPTER 17: REALITY MAY SEEM FINITE, BUT OUR IMAGINATION IS MORE POWERFUL THAN WE KNOW

Babad, E.Y., J. Inbar, and R. Rosenthal. "Pygmalion, Galatea, and the Golem: Investigations of Biased and Unbiased Teachers." *APA PsychNet*. American Psychological Association. *Journal of Educational Psychology* 74, no. 4: 459–474. doi: 10.1037/0022-0663.74.4.459.

Bergland, Christopher. "Imagination Can Change Perceptions of Reality." *Psychology Today*, June 28, 2013. Accessed June 1, 2020. https://www.psychologytoday.com/us/blog/the-athletes-way/201306/imagination-can-change-perceptions-reality.

Bethune, Sophie. "Gen Z More Likely to Report Mental Health Concerns." *Monitor on Psychology*. American Psychological Association 1, vol. 50 (January 2019). https://www.apa.org/monitor/2019/01/gen-z.

Dean, Jeremy. "One Personality Trait Is at the Heart of Many Anxiety Disorders." *PsyBlog,* November 21, 2016. Accessed June 3, 2020. https://www.spring.org.uk/2016/11/personality-trait-anxiety-disorders.php?omhide=true.

"Facts & Statistics," Anxiety and Depression Association of America. Accessed June 2, 2020. https://adaa.org/about-adaa/pressroom/facts-statistics.

"Imagination Can Affect Sight, Sound Senses: Study." Majlis-e-Ulama-e-Shia (Europe). Accessed May 31, 2020. https://majlis.org.uk/imagination-can-affect-sight-sound-senses-study/.

Keogh, Rebecca, and Joel Pearson. "Mental Imagery and Visual Working Memory." PLOS ONE, December 14, 2011. Accessed June 2, 2020. https://journals.plos.org/plosone/article?id=10.1371/journal.pone.0029221.

Marshall, Lisa. "Your Brain on Imagination: It's a Lot like the Real Thing, Study Shows." *CU Boulder Today.* University of Colorado Boulder, December 6, 2018. Accessed May 31, 2020. https://www.colorado.edu/today/node/31511.

"The Pygmalion Effect in the Classroom." *Philonotes. com.* PHILO, October 19, 2019. Accessed June 1, 2020. https://philonotes.com/index.php/2019/10/19/pygmalion-effect/.

Stearns, Peter N. "The History of Happiness." *Harvard Business Review,* October 08, 2014. Accessed June 2, 2020. https://hbr.org/2012/01/the-history-of-happiness.

CHAPTER 18: WE WANT TO CONFORM TO "BEING BUSY," BUT SOCIALIZATION IS OUR SOURCE OF HAPPINESS

Diener, Ed, and M.E.P. Seligman. "Very Happy People." *eddiener.com*, 2002. Accessed June 5, 2020. https://eddiener.com/articles/986.

"The Happiness Lab with Dr. Laurie Santos: For Whom the Alarm Clock Tolls." Pushkin Industries. Apple Podcasts, May 24, 2020. Accessed June 6, 2020. https://podcasts.apple.com/us/podcast/for-whom-the-alarm-clock-tolls/id147424-5040?i=1000475632301.

McLeod, Saul. "Solomon Asch - Conformity Experiment." *Simply Psychology*, last modified December 28, 2018. Accessed June 5, 2020. https://www.simplypsychology.org/asch-conformity.html.

Milyavskaya, Marina, Mark Saffran, Nora Hope, and Richard Koestner. "Fear of Missing Out: Prevalence, Dynamics, and Consequences of Experiencing FOMO." *Motivation and Emotion* 42 (March 17, 2018): 725–737. https://link.springer.com/article/10.1007/s11031-018-9683-5.

Mozes, Alan. "'I'm Just Too Busy' — Is Being Overworked the New Status Symbol?" *Health Day News*. MedicineNet, April 13, 2017. Accessed June 4, 2020. https://www.medicinenet.com/script/main/art.asp?articlekey=202848.

Norton, Michael, and Elizabeth W. Dunn. "Conversation Class." *Princeton Conversation Group* (blog), May 15, 2014. Accessed

June 6, 2020. https://princetonconversationgroup.wordpress.
com/category/conversation-class/.

Vaynshteyn, Gina. "Work Guilt' Is Real and It's Keeping You from
Using Your Vacation Days." Priceline Press Center, October
28, 2019. Accessed June 5, 2020. https://press.priceline.com/
work-guilt-is-real-and-its-keeping-you-from-using-your-va-
cation-days/.

**CHAPTER 19: STEP ON THE CRACKS, APPRECIATE THE
WORLD, AND KEEP THE OIL ON THE SPOON**

Coelho, Paulo. *The Alchemist*. 25th ed. New York: Harper Collins,
2014.

9 781636 764078